Law Practice
STRATEGY

CREATING A NEW BUSINESS MODEL
FOR SOLOS AND SMALL FIRMS

DONNA SEYLE

ISBN: 0615435254
ISBN-13: 9780615435251
Library of Congress Control Number: 2011920026

ACKNOWLEDGEMENTS

Much of the information in this book has been compiled from thoughts, facts and ideas of many who have come before me in the study of law practice trends and technology. I am grateful beyond words to Stephanie Kimbro, Richard Granat, Jordan Furlong, Pam Woldow, Ari Kaplan, Jay Shepherd, Ron Baker, Grant Griffiths, Adrian Dayton, Niki Black, Carolyn Elefant, Lisa Solomon, Susan Cartier Liebel, Kevin Houchin and so many others. They have inspired me to use my time, energy and resources to reach out to those lawyers who struggle to complete and stay informed of critical events in the legal industry.

But of course I could do none of this without the constant support of my husband Nick, who puts up with all my whims; my sons, Taylor and Colin, who have now reached the age when they tell me I need to act mine; my life-long friends Diane and Cathy, who confirm that age has nothing to do with behavior; and my siblings, Eileen, Jeffrey and James, who love me even though I know they're rolling their eyes at me on the other end of the phone.

TABLE OF CONTENTS

CHAPTER 1

THE NEW LEGAL PROFESSION: EMBRACING CHANGE TO PROSPER AS A SOLO OR SMALL FIRM

When I graduated from law school, there were systems in place to point us in a direction. That was way back in 1987, when systems still seemed reliable and functioned well for those who were amenable to them. In law, that included about 95 percent of us. That other 5 percent were brilliant and rebellious and made names for themselves in spite of those three years of sustained indoctrination.

But systems were good for the rest of us, because without them, we wouldn't have had a clue about what to do when you show up in court, let alone how to start a law practice. One way was to clerk at a large or mid-size firm and get an offer of employment once you passed the bar. That way you'd have work until you got hired. This took longer for some than for others.

Law clerking in a firm prepared you for how to practice law, as opposed to just learning the legal theory they taught in law school. It was like an apprenticeship in the law firm lifestyle and kept you from making a fool of yourself when you finally got to stand up before a judge on your own. You never really needed to think about the actual business of law practice until a few years down the road, when the word "partnership" started to creep into the back of your brain (and hopefully into theirs). Although you were always weighed down by the need to create enough billable hours to meet or exceed the firm's expectations, the partnership track was really what motivated you to pay attention to your personal bottom-line contributions to the firm's financial success. It was a logical system.

Having been a paralegal and law clerk for five years before and during law school, I thought anyone who hung out their shingle right out of law school was a fool, unless they had prior clerking experience. You could pick them out in a minute: their suits didn't fall well off their shoulders. Their shoes were not polished. And—my personal favorite—they never knew which side of the courtroom to go to when their motion was called by the judge. But I was young and arrogant and practicing in Los Angeles. To me, appearances were everything.

Still, there were systems even for solos. You sought out local lawyer friends to learn what resources you'd need (the list was fairly simple and straightforward), joined your local bar association, jumped into the yellow pages, and gathered enough cash to keep yourself alive for about a year. You found a respectable office in a suite shared with other attorneys who collectively employed a receptionist, conference room and (a must have) library. There were opportunities to interact and learn from the others about procedures, norms, etiquette, and other important factors never discussed in school. Your dad called all his friends in town and told them you were in business. You joined networking groups and handed out business cards. You picked up overflow work now and again from your network. Eventually, satisfied clients referred their friends to you, and soon you were on your way.

Wow. What year was that again?

Now it's 2011, and the whole world has turned upside down. The law firm business model, just like the financial, health-care, and political models, has broken down. And for those of you whose offers of employment were retracted or delayed, who didn't get an offer (and can't believe it), and who were laid off—there are no systems to follow. Because, truth be told, there is no overflow work anymore. Everybody's just trying to stay alive.

There's lots of activity; lots of talk about technology and blogging and social-media marketing and alternative fee agreements. But there's no tradition, no follow-the-footprints designs or strategies. There is only: this looks good or important or useful, but how does it all fit in? And, by the way, what do I do next?

But you will never know what to do next if you don't understand why the old way no longer works. If you don't stay current with events in the legal industry, you'll never know how to respond in a way that will make you successful.

I have spent the last several years researching, networking in, and blogging about the legal profession and its future, the influences of the economy, technology, globalization, and social media and the solutions that are offered to those who sit where you sit. The result is my strategy to integrate and use solutions that will replace systems that no longer work, and to guide you to a successful solo practice or small firm, for very little cost.

The strategy leads you to where the clients are, shows you how to engage and convert them, and enables you to keep your legal spend low, so that you can offer your services for fixed prices that both you and your clients can afford. All this is done in a way that not only distinguishes your law practice structure, but defines your goals as a lawyer as well.

This strategy is a system to start up or reorganize your practice. It also engages you in the concepts and processes of the evolving practice of law. It is an exciting journey that opens doors to challenges and innovative solutions in this time of professional revolution.

1. THE PROACTIVE LAWYER

In the *Wall Street Journal* article, "Tough Times for Big Law" (December 14, 2009), Elizabeth Wurtzel reported that at the firm of Cravath, Swaine & Moore, a class of associates was asked to delay their hire for one year. In return for the delay, they would receive $80,000 salary, plus benefits and student loan payments—to do nothing. The surprise? Most of the grads turned the offer down.

It really does make you wonder what exactly their decision-making process is based on. Cravath, after all, is one of the most financially sound law firms in the country. They're not going anywhere. Was that their concern? Or did they decide to hold out for a better offer? In this economy?

Or was it really that they were just so red-hot ready to spend the next three to five years of their lives grinding away for ten to twelve hours a day researching and drafting legal documents?

I suspect, as did the author, that it had to do with the fact that their brains had been so dulled by indoctrination and regimentation that they just couldn't conceive of what else they would do with their time. All they could see was themselves, slaving over a lavish desk in their own office with the secretary outside their door and a window behind them that they never looked out of. A fairly narrow vision.

For the majority of law students and lawyers, this is simply not the state of the legal profession today. Yes, it is for some, and always will be. But those numbers have dwindled rapidly, replaced either by desperate job-seekers who don't understand that simple attendance at a top-rated school just doesn't cut it anymore, or by wide-eyed, tech-savvy social networkers who have researched the dynamics of the new law practice environment and are excited about the ride.

There is general agreement among researchers, writers, and thought leaders that a legal mind and an entrepreneurial mind function quite differently. In the article "The Lawyer as Entrepreneur," published by the New Jersey Technology Council, the writers state:

At first glance, lawyers and entrepreneurs don't have much in common. Much like accounting or medicine, many lawyers choose the law as a profession because it offers a low-risk (if high-stress) means to a long, relatively well-paid, and tightly-controlled career at a privately-held law firm or government position. Some even characterize the law as fundamentally antithetical to the entrepreneurial endeavor. Take, for example, Carleton S. Fiorina, the president and chief executive of Hewlett-Packard. In comments to the New York Times profile, Fiorina, who dropped out of UCLA's law school after one semester, noted that she left the law because she could not accept the idea of continually adhering to precedent. Her point was not lost on the Times, which credited Fiorina as a someone who rose to the top by virtue of her willingness to defy the norms of the traditionally male-dominated world of high-tech business.

The lawyer's mind is quite comfortable following the path that is laid out for him or her, substantively, procedurally, and professionally. The entrepreneurial mind is one constantly looking for an innovative (and hopefully better) way to do things.

But while the substantive and procedural rules remain, the professional path is no longer straight and narrow. Pummeled by technology, globalization, and the recession, a lawyer's place in the professional world is no longer guaranteed, and we are now forced to look outside of the box that appeared so secure and comfortable.

The key to surviving, and in fact thriving, today is to change your thinking. We're no longer required to color inside the lines. In fact, there are no longer any lines on the page. Instead, the vision of what you will do in your life must now come from inside you. So many of us followed the path created by images and illusions of life as a lawyer. Now we must create those images ourselves. And because they will be based on what comes from within, they will not be illusions. They will be reflections of who we are and how we can manifest ourselves in the profession we have chosen.

In a wonderful webinar conversation with Kevin Houchin, lawyer and founder of The Space Between Center, he put it like this:

> *The tools are out there to create something for ourselves. Often people are drawn to the legal profession because it provides respect and security. We must now consciously redefine what security and respect mean in a new economy. We must accept the freedom, dig deep into the core of ourselves and find what we know we are very good at, what we love, and put together the tools to enable us to share those things, and people will pay us for that.*

It is not what we expected, not what we worked for, but it is what we have been given. And the opportunities are as numerous as the bounds of our thinking will allow.

And what ARE some of those opportunities? Read what Susan Cartier Liebel, founder of Solo Practice University, says in her blog post entitled "When Large Law Firms Underestimate Lower Cost Rivals, You Win!"

As more solos appear in the market place fighting for their own livelihoods and presenting viable, less expensive alternatives for clients (not necessarily less profitable) and do so more quickly through the use of technology, collaboration, effective use of social media and competitive intelligence available for free on the internet, they will slowly and then more quickly chip away at the market share of big law firms. It's inevitable.

This marketplace is presenting opportunities never really available before because of client demand for lower costs without sacrificing quality (although there are clients comfortable with "good enough") and available low-cost tools for solos to provide these services without sacrificing ethics or professionalism. Big Law has never faced this type of competition before from both colleagues they never really considered competition and clients who are fed up. And because slow-moving large law firms can't adjust their corporate philosophies about billable hours, social media and more fast enough even if they wanted to, solos have a striking competitive edge.

One still needs legal advice no matter how you slice it. Good legal advice is where the money will always be. Interpretation of the laws, strong, intelligent advocating for a position can't be duplicated by filling out a form online or having the lay person represent themselves.

So, armed with the concept that adapting to external forces must be met with internal change, let's take a look at where we are and how we got there.

2. THE DRIVING FORCES BEHIND TODAY'S LEGAL PROFESSION

Identifying the forces that have created the conditions under which the legal profession finds itself functioning may be fairly easy. But the actual effects these forces are having may not be all that readily discernable. We will explore this topic, but only to the extent it is relevant to what we really want to get to: how to be successful in the existing environment. In addition, take the time to read the Eversheds Report entitled: "The Law Firm of the 21ˢᵗ Century: The Clients Revolution" if you have any doubt that what we're discussing here is a permanent change in the way law is currently and will continue to be practiced.

The driving forces we will discuss are:
1. Technology
2. The Recession
3. Globalization

Technology is certainly the most impactful. Always an innovator as well as a disrupter, it has crept into the halls, offices, and meeting rooms of big and small business and has made its presence clear by creating economically viable means with which to meet the cost-savings needs of the legal profession. The recession has not only had effects of its own, but has fueled both technology and globalization to help address its negative impact. And globalization, enabled by technology to foster international business collaboration, has given birth to and is now raising legal process outsourcing (LPOs) providers to be fine young citizens of the legal services neighborhood.

TECHNOLOGY

The desire to scratch your head and walk away from the whole technology thing can be strong, especially when it keeps changing. The tech industry is filled with high-strung, brilliant developers addicted to the game of winning, and they just won't stop. To them, there is no such thing as good enough. There is only: how can this be made better, faster, more functional?

In the late 1990s and early 2000s, static websites and desktop software stood front and center as the must-have technology of the day. Law firms and companies started investing in in-house servers and IT personnel to configure and maintain the increasingly complex and prolific number of software applications they used to run their enterprises. Since big law also had a big budget, solos and small law were left lagging behind in software deployment, then were less able to compete in the marketplace of law clients.

The movement from web 1.0 to web 2.0 has, in fact, created a radical shift in how we communicate, how consumers shop, and, as a result, how business is conducted. Since law practice has now joined the ranks of business enterprise, you, too, are invited to the online party. Today we communicate online, consumers shop online, businesses sell online. And increasingly, as time passes, lawyers practice law online. That's where your clients are, and that's where they expect you to be.

Unfortunately, solos and small firms have lagged behind big law in integrating web 2.0 into their practice. As a result, big law is ahead in this arena, but not for long. Cloud computing developers are falling over each other vying for a piece of your pie, that is, 2.0 applications designed specifically for solo and small firms. And there are some incredibly great products out there for you.

There are many advantages to starting up, or moving your practice to the web 2.0 level (also called eLawyering, cloud computing, virtual law practice), and the effort required to do so is far outweighed by those advantages. Let's take a look at them:

1. That's where your clients are looking for you;
2. That's where your referral sources are;
3. That's where your opportunities to distinguish yourself are;
4. That's where your competition is;
5. It's extremely cost-effective;
6. It creates opportunities for collaboration; and
7. It levels the playing field with big law because it is so affordable

So as much as you might like to return to the "good old days" when all you had to do was sit through a Continuing Legal Education (CLE) class on real property law updates for 2010 (would you really?), there's a whole new world of information out there you need to learn, digest, and implement if you want to succeed in today's legal marketplace.

There are two separate categories of 2.0 you need to learn:

1. Social media: dynamic, content-driven websites, social networking channels, and legal network communities; and

2. Practice management tools: virtual law office (or eLawyering) platforms and document assembly services; or, if you choose to take only a portion of your practice online, there are project, practice, case, time, document, communication, and trial management tools, or any combination of these

Web 2.0 has also raised concerns which affect lawyers more than the general public because of our duty to protect client data. Security and ethical obligations are being addressed state by state, as well as by the American Bar Association. Ethical guidelines and state bar opinions are coming forward slowly, but lag far behind the issues arising as a result of the use of 2.0 media and applications.

Nonetheless, the 2.0 world is here to stay and is necessary to the success of your practice. You can obtain a great list of categorized web tools by downloading my ebook (free) *Web 2.0 Management Tools for Solos and Small Firms*, at www.LawPracticeStrategy.com/blog

THE RECESSION

In the fall 2008, there was a strange sound reverberating through the halls of venerable law firms across the nation. It was the sound of silence; specifically, telephone silence. Landlines, cell phones, didn't matter. They weren't ringing. The financial avalanche of the failing housing market and the fractured foundations of derivative swaps rolled through the streets of our major metropolitan areas like a tsunami through Bangladesh, devastating investment and commercial banks and bringing credit markets and transactional activity to a halt.

It wasn't just that law clients couldn't afford the legal services they had relied on in the past. It was that they weren't doing anything to *require* legal services. The disappearance of the *need* for legal services is what, for the legal industry, separated this recession from those of the past. And it was this disappearance that generates the question, "Will we return to the past?" not "When will we return to the past?"

The reductions in legal forces were, and continue to be, unprecedented. First came the lay-offs, then the cut-back of new associate hiring, delays in and rescissions of existing employment offers, the rearrangement within firms of partnership tracks, abandonment of "lockstep" hiring practices, cancelled summer programs, reduced hiring goals, and then—the one thing that makes predictions for the future so impossible— the pent-up supply of deferred hires.

Along with this crushing scenario came increased consumer demand for alternative fee arrangements and the resurgence of solos and boutique firms. But no one can come to a consensus as to what will happen next. As the recession abates (if it abates), would law firms be able to resume their traditional practices? Or had this economic downturn produced "a fundamental shift in the legal marketplace?" (See Georgetown Law's

"Law Firm Evolution: Brave New World or Business as Usual?")

That question is still unanswered, although big law is increasingly betting that the answer will be no. New and unemployed lawyers seek alternatives to their plight, and solos and small firms have been their figurative seas of tranquility.

But where do you start? The old brick-and-mortar collegial environment lies at the bottom of the rubble. Clients have become aware of the profession's vulnerability and are refusing to agree to over-the-top, open-ended hourly fee arrangements. A law firm has become a business commodity, with marketing and bottom-line decisions marching ahead of legal ability. Law school graduates and big law refugees were never taught how to run a business, let alone find their way through technology and social media. How does one comprehend all of this? That is what this strategy is designed to help you do.

GLOBALIZATION

Technology is also responsible for spawning a segment of the legal industry mentioned earlier, legal process outsourcing, primarily offshore. Like businesses that contract with foreign labor forces to manufacture goods sold in the US, domestic law firms aregravitating toward LPOs that perform legal support services to reduce costs incertain phases of massive legal projects.

LPOs have flourished primarily in India, where it is expected to be a $20 billion industry by 2015. Outsourcing is cited as one of most significant tools to contain costs, and is thus making its way into the heart of the evolving legal practice format.

LPO providersperform such work as document review, many phases of the ediscovery process, due diligence in a variety of scenarios, and anything that is repetitive or standardized. They now invest in training their law school graduates in foreign law and procedures to better serve their US, UK, and other foreign clients.

Some LPOs have corporate offices in the US to create a domestic presence that gives offshore LPOs a greater perception of legitimacy and therefore, a greater market share The recent purchase of Pangea3, an offshore LPO, by Thomson Reuters has the legal profession holding its breath in anticipation of what will result from the merger of a global leader in outsourcing with the world's largest legal research provider and publisher.

While LPOs present yet another competitor to the already challenged solo/small law market, they also represent a cost containment strategy for those firms as well, assuming the firm has sufficient business of warrant their services.

The LPO trend, however, can be challenged with the adoption of virtual law practice models and legal tech tools because, once again, the firms (your potential client source) that are outsourcing their work to foreign LPOs are comfortable with the online environment.

There is another aspect to globalization that presents opportunities to the technologically sophisticated. My review of emerging technology has shown a growth in the development of collaborative workspaces as an element of many new web 2.0 offerings. As international business proliferates, there is a growing need for foreign and domestic attorneys to work together to negotiate and create contracts that will comply with the requirements of each jurisdiction that are not covered under international law.

Both of these scenarios present new opportunities for the technologically proficient lawyer to tap into sources of business not otherwise available to them. In the present legal marketplace, no lawyer can afford to cut the cord to income sources that can mean the difference between success and failure.

3. THE INEVITABILITY OF INNOVATION

Much has been written and discussed about the reticence with which lawyers approach the massive restructure of business practice as they have come to know it. Law school trains us to make legal arguments by following precedent, to rely on what has been decided before. Almost all lawyers have gone to work at law firms after passing the bar, and learn from an established institution how "things are done." While this is true of other professions as well (e.g., the medical profession—and look at the mess they're in), there is not one profession that is more risk-adverse than law. And since change involves risk, well—you get my point. And as we have seen, lawyers have a lot of change on the table.

In "Innovate Now?" Michael J. Anderson writes:

> *When law firms finally realize that they are falling behind (minimal or non-existent profit*

growth, lower margins and/or declining market share), the first knee jerk reaction is to reduce costs and start to restructure. In law firms that usually means laying off associates and staff. The sad thinking seems to be that since there is little chance that we can increase the total number of billable hours, we had better share those hours among fewer people and those people should be the owners. For some strange reason we choose to keep the people who cost us the most and let go those who cost less and who will provide a better long term and short term future for the firm.

That kind of response to today's economic tsunami is both shortsighted and ineffective. Richard Susskind, a law professor from the UK, revered legal futurist, and author of *The Future of Law* (1996) and *The End of Lawyers?* (2008), has been researching, tracking, and forecasting the effects of technology on the practice of law since the mid 1980s.

In *The End of Lawyers?*, he foresees:

- The path to commoditization, a continuum of kinds of legal services, from bespoke (original documents) to standardized, systematized, packaged and commoditized
- Standardization of recurrent legal tasks
- Systemization of repetitive tasks
- Packaged tasks—giving clients access to a firm's systems so they can do it themselves, but with the availability of attorney input as necessary
- Commoditized products—a completely standardized service that can be made available on a mass basis with little or no attorney input

17

- Proliferation of eLawyering, or virtual law firms, that provide services online

and paradigm shifts that include moving legal services:
- From an advisory service to an information service
- From a reactive service to a proactive service
- From time-based billing to commodity pricing
- From a legal focus to a business focus
- From problem-solving to legal risk management (preemptive consulting rather than litigation)
- From an adversarial to a collaborative practice model

Susskind was the keynote speaker at Georgetown Law's Brave New World Conference in March 2010. At the conference, thought leaders looked at how far these predictions have come to fruition. The presenters not only confirmed that the revolution is here, but emphasized that it is even beyond our expectations. Just as businesses in general have revolutionized their business practices, so law firms will continue to be required to do so if they want to remain viable.

The seriousness of the movement is being taken even further overseas. In a blog post called "The Blind Side," Jordan Furlong, law firm consultant and award-winning blogger who writes about the extraordinary changes underway in the legal profession, states:

> *One of Richard's [Susskind] topics was the Legal Services Act in England & Wales, and its soon-to-be-active provisions allowing alternative business structures (ABSs), including non-lawyer equity investment in law firms and legal enterprises . . .he reported that law firms are not their primary target; in fact, their interest is coalescing around legal service providers that*

we now consider to be on the fringes of the profession, like legal processing outsourcing companies. These are the providers that outside investors think are much likelier than law firms to emerge successful from the ABS upheaval, and it's where most of the new capital is going to go.

The conference also stressed that the nature of LPO projects would grow from "grunt work" to projects of more significance, thereby requiring greater skill levels. The outsourcing of these projects is another cost-effective practice that can increase a large firm's bottom line, but also threatens the need for the traditional associate hire.

A national survey, commissioned by LexisNexis in early 2010, found the following:

- Corporate counsel say law firms are not doing enough to respond to the economic downturn
- Private practice attorneys say clients are too focused on costs, at the expense of quality and results
- Opinions are split on the future of the legal industry and whether the recession will permanently change the way business is done in the legal industry
- The next generation of lawyers feel ill-equipped for the business of law; many are considering alternatives to a career in law

IAn important interview with Susskind entitled "The Mainstream Revolutionary" by Neil Rose of LegalFutures.com:states that:

the recession has crystallised the "underlying commercial imperative" that was starting to take hold two years ago of in-house counsel wanting more for less. "This drive... has been

19

strengthening year on year. And one of the big debates that I discuss in the book is whether or not when the economy returns and the dust settles, we will just revert to fairly high hourly rates and the old tariff essentially. And most law firms and clients I speak to say that's not going to happen. You can't put the toothpaste back in the tube."

In the second part of this interview, "Susskind: Fail to Embrace 'Legal Process Management' and Lose Out to New Players," the author states:

Healthier firms recognise the need "to invest in new ways of undertaking their routine and repetitive legal work at much lower cost than today", Professor Susskind continues, reaffirming the importance he attaches to legal process management. This involves "decomposing" a legal matter into its constituent tasks, and finding the most efficient and appropriate way to carry out each – what he calls "multi-sourcing." He also reflects on how fast legal process outsourcing has developed over the past two years.

The pressure to take a law practice into the twenty-first century, created by technology and pushed urgently along by the recession, is further augmented by emerging consumer expectations. In his paper "Online Legal Services: Future of the Profession," Richard Granat's research reveals that consumers will avoid using lawyers unless absolutely necessary because they can't afford them, don't trust them, don't like paying open-ended hourly fees, and perceive lawyers to be high risk in terms of outcomes and cost/ benefits. He says:

These pressures to change the patterns of delivery of legal services for consumers will increase dramatically in the next few years, as a connected generation comes of age. Whatever trends are now in place will accelerate over the coming years as the connected generation comes of age and matures into the age where they need legal services.

Granat goes on to define connected consumers values:
- Innovation—the better way;
- Immediacy—e.g., I want it now;
- Authentication and trust;
- Interactivity defines the culture;
- High customization—services and products that fit unique needs.

and states that consumer behaviors emphasize:
- Looking to the Internet as the first place to go for information, alternatives, and options;
- Comparison sites are a focus;
- Consumers want to try before they buy;
- Connected consumers look for communities of interest where opinions and information can be exchanged;
- Connected consumers look for digital spaces that are interactive;
- Connected consumers would rather interact with a website before talking to a professional;
- Eventually, consultation with a professional may occur, but only after this digital exploration.

Granat's bottom line is that "[t]he connected generation wants to do business over the Internet with attorneys and intuitively understands the idea of online legal services."

In his paper, "The Evolution of the Legal Profession," Ari Kaplan predicts that future changes will include the following:

- The performance of legal work will be less collegial and more businesslike
- Attorney/client relationships will be formed globally, not locally
- The use of alternative fee agreements will be used to increase business and satisfy consumers
- There will be increased lawyer mobility
- Quality of work will be presumed, and added value will be expected
- Clients will expect lawyers to look proactively for efficient performance options
- Documents and information will be accessed online
- Efficient e-discovery technology will eliminate need for document review
- Clients will refuse to pay for first-year associates
- Law practices will become a competitive business, no longer a "secret science"
- Clients will demand a focus on what can be resolved rather than assume the need for protracted litigation

That's a lot of change, and these changes are not superficial. They penetrate deep into the traditions and legacies of law practice, dragging legal theory down off its analytic pedestal onto the ground where the laymen live. In so doing, the legal process will become more transparent, accountable, and accessible to those who are being served by it. This is a good thing.

In order for new and existing solos and small firms to succeed in this demanding environment, they must incorporate practices that will:
- Reduce costs and compete with technology
- Enable clients to find them online
- Provide services in a manner and at a cost that the consumer will accept
- Become a trustworthy partner with their clients

Obviously, the primary purpose of these changes it to compete efficiently, effectively and successfully in the marketplace. But there is another benefit to you as a lawyer.

All of these practices encourage an openness and engagement with the client that creates a more satisfying experience than we, as lawyers, often encounter. Blogging and engaging in social media with authenticity encourage self-expression, so if a client comes to you via those means, he or she will have a good sense of who you are. Working with clients to come to fee agreements creates a cooperative relationship and eases the anxiety of the billing outcome for both the client and the practitioner. Using technology properly will enable you to think better, work smarter, and get more done with less cost and effort. And the online community is full of vibrant people sharing information and ideas, opportunities to connect with like-minded people across the globe, and their excitement in sharing in the technological revolution that is creating a whole new set of rules to play by.

Jordan Furlong brought into focus yet another profound benefit of our times in his blog post "The Platform is Changing":

> *We can't blame this on the recession anymore—what we're seeing is more fundamental than that. The traditional platform for legal service delivery is giving way, overburdened by its own inefficiencies, inflexibility, and market-unfriendliness. In its place is emerging a new platform — the internet. And on that platform is springing up a multitude of new models by which clients can purchase the legal services they want, whether through virtual or distributed law firms with minimal overhead, advanced software for the completion of simple documents or the facilitation of basic transactions, process-savvy lawyers in other countries or quasi-lawyers in our own jurisdictions, and other platforms yet to emerge that we can't currently envision. The common thread is client customization: the type, quality, and timeliness of service you want at the price you're prepared to pay. Law firms will emerge and compete on these bases as well, but they'll be far from the only game in town.*

A chance to change the inefficiencies, inflexibility and market-unfriendliness of our profession: what a great opportunity! Tomorrow's law firms are already here. It's a great time to be a lawyer, but a confusing time to understand how to create a law practice that will work. Practitioners who succeed need to have a system and a strategy in place.

I have read hundreds of reports, survey results, reviews of national and international societies' meetings, listened to webinars, studied technology, and attended conferences on the contributing factors to the current state of the marketplace, the future of law, and how solos and small firms can survive it. What I found most confusing was that there was no one source that put all of the challenges and their solutions together in one focused strategy to succeed in the midst of such radical change that our profession will never be the same, even in the opinion of the most conservative thinkers.

In a recent panel discussion entitled Defining the Law Firm of the Future, the only point on which there was consensus among all of the thought leaders was this: **"The firm that will thrive in the future is the firm that is able to deliver better value through innovation and technology."**

VALUE. INNOVATION. TECHNOLOGY.

OK, we're ready. What is a system or strategy that will incorporate all the components of a twenty-first-century law practice?

The *Law Society Gazette*'s article "The Best Advice on How to Prepare for a Legal Services Revolution," states that the goal is to "identify a strategy that maximizes … chances of success, whatever the future holds." This requires deciding which part of the market you want to succeed in and, given where you are, determining what you need to do to get there. It includes all the elements of a full business-plan assessment focused on your strengths, weaknesses, your market, and your competition. It requires a customer-focused mindset, the development and use of solid management skills, and capturing the hearts and minds of customers through engagement and communication. Without this mindset, you will not be able to do the rest.

Agreed. But we're lawyers. We need to know what the rules are. We need a blueprint for how to put this endeavor together. I couldn't find one, so I created a strategy for myself, and here it is. The elements of this strategy address every challenge presented by a changing profession and will set you on a course that will enable you to stay ahead of whatever lies around the corner.

So here are our challenges:
- Too few clients who need legal representation can afford it
- Attracting clients in a highly competitive environment
- Increased client expectations: value, cost, and access
- Competition with big law
- Staying abreast of the future of business: technology, collaboration, and globalization

Here are the solutions:
- Offer clients alternative fee agreements
- Employ legal project management principals
- Put your practice in the cloud and use productivity tech tools
- Use content marketing techniques

None of these solutions is a novel idea. All of them have been explored and advocated by professionals in all forms of media, and many of us have read about or explored them to one degree or another.

But here's the key: while viewing each one separately may create interest and a certain amount of enthusiasm, by integrating them into a functional whole wherein each solution contributes to the efficacy of the others, a strategy of how they work together to create a successful practice begins to emerge.

Let's take a quick look at the solutions before we talk about how they address each of the challenges.

1. <u>Legal Project Management</u>. Project management is a fancy term for a system of analyzing needs and actions, prioritizing, organizing, and being held accountable. It has become a relatively complex and highly refined skill used to execute business processes and is now being tapped as the number one method to create efficiency in your law practice. The practice of law, in fact, fits quite nicely into a project management system, as there are specific actions, deadlines, and other aspects of a legal matter that can be easily mapped out within a PM framework. It also works well in conjunction with assessing fixed pricing up front, as it requires that you identify and map out each step of the legal matter at the outset and then execute according to that plan.

2. <u>Content Marketing</u>. Notice I did not say "social media marketing." Because although content marketing is achieved through the use of social media, it is really about creating an online presence that reflects your desire to educate and to keep your clients informed. It is accomplished by researching and blogging about important substantive topics directed at your target market in a way that will engage them, invite them to comment and hopefully create a conversation

among your readers. By doing so, you build your voice of authority and bring people and concepts togethe. It involves active engagement in social media, networking, and syndication. Yes, you must be on LinkedIn, Facebook, and Twitter. They each serve a different function, and work in conjunction with your blog to bolster your online presence. For lawyers, there are also several must-participate sites that we will discuss in Chapter 4 on content marketing.

3. <u>Virtual Law Offices and Legal Technology Resources</u>. There are many choices of how, and to what degree, to use web 2.0, or cloud computing, services to manage your practice. From research tools to trial-preparation and mobile applications, free and low cost web-based resources are also available to you as cost- and time-saving systems. The efficiency and cost savings of this expanding business model are no longer in question, but there are also security and ethics issues which must be addressed in the decision-making process. Security issues around web 2.0 technology may challenge your comfort zone, but its use is inevitable and represents a cost reduction that is essential to success in the current and evolving law practice environment.

4. <u>Alternative Fee Agreements</u>. Every thought leader in the industry agrees that the billable hour fee structure no longer works in the current legal marketplace due to economic conditions and client demands. In fact, it creates a conflict of interest between attorneys and clients which will be discussed at length in Chapter 7. Even big law is incorporating alternative

billing methods into their systems in order to retain clients who will no longer agree to pay on the traditional open-ended, hourly fee basis. Value-based pricing and other models are quickly being developed, explored, and implemented by firms large and small. You must begin to incorporate variable fee structures into your practice for your clients, your business, and yourself.

Now let's look at how these solutions address each of the challenges we face in this new economic and technological world:

1. <u>Too few clients can afford lawyers</u>: how do you make your services available to them?
   - Alternative pricing models shifts the risk of cost of representation from the client to the attorney, thereby alleviating the anxiety of an open-ended price tag on your services. You can work with clients to create a pricing plan that will work for both of you.

2. <u>Attracting clients in a competitive environment</u>: how do you stand out from the crowd?
   Content marketing gets you found online, where the clients are and where they expect you to be, and provides a method of branding yourself and your practice, connecting with your target client base, creating a relationship with your target client base through value-added content, and creating a community of followers who will not only use your services, but also refer you to their friends and family. It enables you to continue contact with your clients even after representation is complete,

without any extra effort, and to keep you front and center in their minds.

- Alternative pricing models is an added value for your clients and prospective clients, acting as a very subtle marketing tool to engage your target market by offering alternatives which directly affect their choice of representation.

3. <u>Increased client expectations</u>: how can you offer them value, access, and reduced costs?

- Content marketing keeps you visible online and offers clients an ongoing source of information that is valuable to them, at no cost. They know that each time they receive something from you, whether via email or through social networks, it will benefit them.

- Alternative pricing models meets your clients' expectations that you will do your best work to achieve the best result at a controlled cost.

- eLawyering (using virtual law office technology, other cloud and mobile applications, or any combination) meets clients' expectations of virtual interaction and offers them immediate access to you, rather than creating a string of exchanged phone calls or arranging face-to-face meetings when these are not absolutely necessary. Your clients are just as busy as you are. Virtual communication has created the ability and thus the desire to minimize time spent exchanging information. You client has access to all written communications and all documents in the case through a simple online interface on your website. If they have questions for you, they can email them and know they will receive a response within whatever time frame you establish by your policy.

4. <u>Compete with big law by reducing overhead</u>.

    - Content marketing, eLawyering, and adopting efficient project management principles all reduce your overhead significantly. The costs of traditional marketing techniques, staffing, and running a brick and mortar office can be reduced, and in some cases eliminated, by taking advantage of social media and emerging technologies that are there to support these efforts and which are expanding at a rapid pace.

    - Cost containment enables you as a solo or small firm to compete with big law in attracting and retaining clients, thereby leveling the playing field and offering an opportunity for solos and small or boutique firms to drive the direction of the legal profession by their aggregate success.

    - The ability to incorporate these methods into your practice has added benefits, primarily by freeing you to comfortably meet clients' expectations with regard to pricing their representation. Bearing the risk of fixed fees or other alternative arrangements is easily undertaken when your cost controls manage your bottom line.

    - As you can see, the elements of this management strategy work in conjunction with one another to address the challenges of starting or restructuring your firm. Not only does it create solutions, but it also defines a law practice that allows both lawyer and client to enjoy working together in partnership toward a resolution, rather than pursuing an adversarial and expensive course of action. It sets the stage for creating a long-term relationship focused on proactive risk avoidance rather than reactive problem-solving. It is a strategy that enables you to break free of the constraints of traditional law firm practice that are often unpleasant and unproductive.

CHAPTER 2

COST CONTAINMENT, EFFICIENCY, AND PROJECT MANAGEMENT

1. WHY CONTAIN COSTS?

At this point, it's no secret that if the traditional law firm business model had to compete in the business world, it would fail miserably. Never before have law firms needed to think about containing costs and working efficiently. In fact, as we will see in the section on alternative fee arrangements, efficiency in creating work product is actually not in the lawyer's or law firms' best interest. And creating reasonable work-flow processes and using the right tools to get the job done quickly were just not in the law firm's production manual.

Traditional firms are resistant to these changes because they are afraid: afraid of the unknown and afraid to take risks. Since law firms have never been efficient or cost-effective, their fears are probably well-founded. They have gotten away with raising their hourly rates year after year, almost without considering their costs.

Now, law practices must align their business models with standard business theory based on efficiency, cost-effectiveness and the bottom line. They are losing clients who have suffered as a result of the recession and can no longer afford to take on uncertain and overpriced legal fees. This is the perfect opportunity for solos and small, boutique firms to draw those clients away from traditional firms by creating a business model that enables them to meet clients' demands and expectations.

Again, in "How to Compete on Price," Jordan Furlong gives us the following examples:

- ***Install a legal project management system.*** *Probably the simplest way to introduce business efficiencies to your law firm is to <u>adopt the principles of legal project management</u>. From a basic back-of-the-envelope process for doing certain tasks systematically all the way up to a full-scale Lean Six Sigma re-engineering of your entire operation, you'll wind up with clearer goals, more explicit processes, more efficient systems and increased productivity.*

- ***Automate anything repetitive that moves.*** *Your client intake system, your most frequent inquiries, your most common procedures, your most familiar routines: if the same basic task occurs more than occasionally in your firm, it should be converted into a template, a checklist, a document assembly system, or some other means by which completion is made faster, variation is made more difficult, and fewer resources are expended needlessly.*

- ***Move work up and down the talent chain.*** *Move dictation and transcription from secretaries down* *to voice-recognition devices. Move legal research to freelance specialists across town or outside the country. Move administrative tasks to virtual assistants. Move e-discovery to people or systems actually qualified to do it. Then train the people who used to do low-value work in high-value skills like project management, business development, human resources and so forth. Same people, same resources, but better allocated and with new capabilities.*

- ***Use technology wherever possible.*** *Practice management software, on your server or preferably <u>in the cloud</u>, delivers huge efficiency gains. Specialized accounting software for law offices reduces errors and improves productivity. Take advantage of low-cost, internet-based contact management systems. Give serious thought to going paperless, or at least paper-less. If you're already using these tools, constantly train your staff to become more proficient with them. Exploit what <u>Dave Bilinsky</u> calls the "new leverage": using technology to achieve higher rates of return on each hour of work.*

While some of these suggestions don't apply when you're starting up your firm, they contain the general concepts of cost containment. Clearly, automation is your friend, and while the move to refer some legal products as "commodities" is not always well-received among attorneys, we've been commoditizing our work product for years without thinking about it (remember the "forms" files on our C-drives?). Now, technology has developed applications that do that for us, making it yet even less costly to produce a document.

2. USING LEGAL PROJECT MANAGEMENT SYSTEMS

Project management is actually a very simple concept based on common sense. It is the systemization of a project, and people do it all the time. However, when the project involves hundreds of contributors ranging over numerous geographic areas who frequently don't know each other, it can quickly get complicated. As the world got smaller, it became necessary to create high-level systems to handle these scenarios.

A project has a budget and a deadline, as well as a series of events that must occur in a particular order. The practice of project management has been developed by the business community to create a workflow blueprint to prioritize, design, and coordinate a detailed plan to reach the project's goal efficiently, on schedule, and on budget. These systems are clearly beneficial to law practice, where each matter, motion, or contract could be a project. Think about how helpful it would be to have a blueprint to follow for drafting or responding to a summary judgment motion, negotiating and drafting a fifty-page commercial lease, or preparing for trial.

In each scenario, the process can be broken down intp steps, assigned, calendared, and monitored to avoid work reproduction, oversights, or mistakes and create accountability. At the end of the project, you and your team can review the process to see what worked or didn't, and change your blueprint for the future. Over time, the efficiency created by tracking the process will drive your costs down and your quality and profits up. By including your client in the process landmarks, your work becomes more transparent and your client relationship is strengthened. Pam Woldow, in her blog post "Stop Complaining & DO Something!" says this:

> *There is an enormous need for a more orderly, rational and cost-effective approach to providing legal services. It's hardly surprising that firms and enlightened legal departments are embracing Legal Project Management (LPM)— which offers a disciplined approach for planning, controlling and executing a legal matter within the constraints of time, budget and agreed-upon performance requirements.*

> *This also is why those law firms that are adopting LPM have the chance to outdistance their disorderly, inefficient competitors in the highly-competitive legal services market. Clients may still feel they lack the leverage to beat back law firm rate increases, but when it comes to an approach for driving more value into service as LPM does, they know when they are being offered a good thing.*

Unfortunately, efficiency has never been what practicing law was all about. Researching, pondering, and brainstorming in a collegial environment was more the idea, and I guess when when lawyers were serving the captains of industry and burgeoning corporate domains, could afford to do that. That practice model modernized, but otherwise did not change all that much over the centuries. As Jordan Furlong, in "How I Learned to Stop Worrying and Love Project Management," puts it:

*... we lawyers pride ourselves on our capacity for ingenuity: the unexpected insight that makes a deal possible, the brilliant argument that turns a trial around, the stroke of inspiration that not only saves the day but also shows off just how bright we are ... At some level, we take offence at the idea of project management because it seems to reduce this wonderful profession of ours to little more than a series of steps, a collection of flow charts that **anyone** could follow.*

Lawyers think of themselves as intellectual warriors with every right to get paid (in many cases) obscene amounts of money for their talents. But as with the saying about war—"What if they had a war and nobody came?"—law firms have recently come face to face with the reality that just because they have a law firm doesn't mean the clients will come.

Not only is efficiency never rewarded in the traditional model, but efficiency's opposite, billable hours, are. In "Are Law Firms Really Ready for Project Management?" William Henderson observes:

... project management requires a fundamentally different mindset than the traditional time and materials model. Planning is far and away the most time consuming activity, and it is typically done through lengthy team meetings to solicit the best ideas, create buy-in, and ensure optimal coordination and communication. Further, the ROI on project management comes over time as the workforce climbs the learning curve. This approach is fundamentally at

odds with the billable hour silos that produced high profits for so many years. For project management to work in law firms, management is going to have to change incentives away from billable hours and toward profitable projects and satisfied clients.

This will not be an easy transition. And the more entrenched the firm is in tradition, the harder it will be. This is why solos and boutique firms have such an advantage over big firms: they can start up or change their business model quickly, thereby giving them more immediate access to clients who are learning to love fixed pricing, constant access to files, and engagement in their legal process. The expectations of today's clients cannot be met by traditional practices. Once again, I must quote from Jordan Furlong in "How I Learned to Stop Worrying and Love Project Management":

The day of the haphazard lawyer, who pursues a solution by intuition, experience and the loosest possible timetable, is drawing to a close. In his place is emerging the process-driven lawyer: disciplined, procedural and systematic, who understands that madness lies not in method, but in its absence.

Think about how your clients would react if, rather than taking all their paperwork, reviewing the details of their matter and then taking action (without their understanding or concern for cost), you reviewed the documentation, created a workflow analysis of the necessary and alternative actions, possible outcomes, and a budget to match different scenarios. Then you met with your client to review the plan, define your goals, choose performance pathways and determine the value of your services. Suddenly, the entire nature of the attorney/client relationship changes. And this is the way clients now expect and demand that their lawyers engage with them.

The legal project management system you or your firm will use can be either custom-created or follow one of several offshoots of the formal project management systems training required for certification. Particularly for solos and small firms, it does not need to be complex, but it does need to include several essential elements as well as the dedication to spend the time and energy necessary to create, use, and revise it along the way. A list of necessary steps in developing a project management system is:

- Devise an easy system of communication among you, the team, and the client
- Specify the scope and objectives of the project with your clients—determine their desired outcomes or acceptable alternatives
- List the specific actions that will be required or that may arise
- Create a timeline and schedule to track due dates and strategic actions
- Determine how long it will take to complete each part of the project
- Decide who will be a part of the team and assign specific tasks within the project
- Plan meetings, follow-up, or other methods to monitor each player's progress

The tech industry follows a system called Agile, which uses the following framework:

- Practice #1: Guiding Vision—establish a guiding vision for the project and continuously reinforce it through words and actions
- Practice #2: Teamwork & Collaboration—facilitate collaboration and teamwork through relationships and community
- Practice #3: Simple Rules—establish and support the team's set of guiding
- practices
- Practice #4: Open Information—provide open access to information
- Practice #5: Light Touch—apply just enough control to foster emergent order
- Practice #6: Agile Vigilance—constantly monitor and adjust

There are dozens of project management software and cloud products that you can choose to build a digital environment to work in.

3. USING CLOUD PRODUCTIVITY TOOLS

There are two separate purposes that web 2.0 tools can help you accomplish: marketing and management. Since both your clients and your competitors are online, your visibility is essential and can be successfully accomplished through the strategic use of social media, which will be discussed in the section on content marketing. Here, we will focus on productivity tools to help you use your time more efficiently.

The realm of legal technology is a multi-faceted discussion and includes the theoretical implications of its use as well as the effects on the nature of law practice itself. It involves the definition of a virtual law office, the technology behind it, the available choices to be made, and the legal implications of its use. It also includes the various practice models available, what they actually do, and which ones would be best suited for various types of law practices. But most importantly, it has sparked a call for a redefinition of the practice of law versus the delivery of legal services, including a very heated debate over whether a law degree is necessary to perform legal service functions.

HOW TECHNOLOGY IS AFFECTING THE PRACTICE OF LAW

The legal technology available to us today is staggering, not just in amount but in functionality, and we are only seeing the tip of the iceberg. Technology is no longer limited to software that sits on a desktop, processing functions. It has revolutionized work systems by adding versatility, intelligence, and interactivity to its arsenal. It has literally broken down the barriers of space and time in such a way that old business models and systems, including those of law firms, can no longer compete in today's marketplace without integrating progressive technology systems into their business models.

Technology has revolutionized the way we receive information. Print media is suffering for good reason: they charge for their media and they're yesterday's news. On the other hand, electronic information is instantaneously available in the comfort of wherever you happen to want it, and mostly it is free.

Technology has, of course, radically changed the way we communicate. Mobile phones are predominantly used for texting, and interaction takes place on our social network channels, where we have opportunities to connect with people irrespective of their location in the world. The value of such opportunities for society has yet to be seen; but from a personal perspective, I confess I am enthralled with the connections I have been able to establish as a participant in this truly brave new world. The effort in communication systems has turned expectations upside-down: where before it was burdensome to learn to use these technologies, it is now burdensome to try to reach someone by voice phone or in person.

And it doesn't stop there. There is real movement, begun decades ago in the study of artificial intelligence, toward the development and use of knowledge tools. In his mind-boggling book, *The Lawyer's Guide to Working Smarter with Knowledge Tools*, Marc Lauritsen states:

> *The ability of software to do things acknowledged as "smart" also has been on the rise. Artificial intelligence and expert systems go way back, even though practical applications have been slow in coming. In the legal world we now have online inferencing systems (like Jnana) and Web-based document assembly*

tools (like DealBuilder, Exari, and HotDocs) that can embody a great deal of know-how and perform complex analytical and text-generation tasks. Knowledge-based applications enable dynamic, interactive user experiences and increasingly do valuable intellectual labor. Online advisors step people through important decisions and activities; intelligent templates assemble both simple documents and elaborate sets.

In other words, technology can research, analyze, and make decisions for us as well. The productivity, responsiveness, quality of work, consistency, and the reduction of much of the tediousness of law practice that these systems create for us transforms the nature of our practice in fundamental ways.

A great example of this is contained in the marketing/management application recently launched by RealPractice.com called MyRealPractice. This software as a service (Saas) product includes an alerts function that gets smarter as you use the program. As you enter data and use its functionality in both managing your matters and marketing your firm, the alert section on your dashboard will advise you of best-practices ideas to create increased efficiency and marketing effectiveness.

It's important to gain perspective on the direction this march to progress is taking. These systems, because of their efficiency, are being embraced by businesses large and small. Law firms lag behind primarily because the profession does not see itself as a business. But given the effects of market forces on the profession, we all need to get the wake-up call: any entity that has as one of its objectives making money is a business, and needs to start operating as such if it wants to survive.

Efficiency is the goal; technology is an essential means to attain it.

THE MOVEMENT FROM LEGACY SOFTWARE TO WEB 2.0 APPLICATIONS

In the PP-LTI (Perfect Practice Legal Technology Institute) study conducted by the Legal Technology Institute, University of Florida Levin School of Law, the authors found that there was a failure of small law professionals to adopt even the simplest technologies, such as document management systems. The study indicated that 52 percent of all surveyed did not use technology at all. Eighty percent of the respondents who reported using a document management system were from large firms. Sixty-one percent of small firms said they did not use metadata cleanup software, and of the 25 percent of respondents who reported using email encryption, only 20 percent were at small firms.

Routing and notifications of paperless workflow were much more prevalent at large firms. Only 50 percent of small firms reported using a practice management system versus nearly 83 percent of large firms.

Non-users reported cost and an inability to see the benefits of technology as the main factors in failing to adopt technology in their firms. Interestingly, those who cited cost as a reason estimated the cost to be more than double the actual price of the technology.

As cloud computing developers expand the possibilities of web 2.0 functions, there is a huge movement by big and small business, governments, agencies, schools, and institutions of all kinds away from desktop applications and into the cloud. In a recent survey of approximately 900 internet and tech experts and social analysts, Elon University and the Pew Research Center came to this conclusion:

> *By 2020, most people won't do their work with software running on a general-purpose PC. Instead, they will work in Internet-based applications such as Goggle Docs, and in applications run from smartphones. Aspiring application developers will develop for smartphone vendors and companies that provide internet-based applications, because most innovative work will be done in that domain, instead of designing applications that run on a PC operating system.*

Innovation in cloud technology now predominates practice management systems, enabling not just law practice management or matter-management functions, but also the integration of project management and collaboration modules. The choice of what kind of tools you use depends on the specific needs of your practice.

WHAT DO YOU NEED TO START OUT?

There are web 2.0 applications and Saas products that do everything from create efficiency to help develop legal arguments. They function much like Saas VLOs, which will be discussed in a later chapter. Modeled on the monthly subscription basis, they require no purchase, but some do require a modest monthly subscription cost. Others are completely free. They help you organize, manage, brainstorm, track time, communicate, collaborate, research, assemble, store, search, and distribute documents and prepare for trial in secured environments. To the extent these functions are not included in your VLO choice, they are here to back you up for free or minimal cost. Some of the most popular categories are:

- Mindmapping applications help you brainstorm and organize your thoughts, visualize all aspects of your litigation, simplify complex information, capture, organize, and annotate your legal research and manage your tasks more effectively.
- Use project management/collaboration products when you need a more comprehensive solution than a to-do list. They include file sharing, message boards, communication functions, milestones, and time-tracking for specific projects such as handling a summary judgment motion or preparing for trial. These kinds of tools will become even more essential as law practice moves toward collaboration and away from confrontation.
- You can conduct web meetings, manage long-term negotiations in secured deal rooms, and

manage group discussions in virtual workspaces and deal rooms.

I have compiled a comprehensive list of web 2.0 applications, categorized by function, in my e-book *Web 2.0 Tools for Lawyers*, available free at http://www.LawPracticeStrategy.com. Many of your choices will depend on which, if any, kind of VLO you choose. The more comprehensive the platform you choose, the fewer of these applications you will find useful. Sometimes you will find the need to use an application only for a limited time. That's fine since most of these tools have no long-term commitment requirement.

Some of the tools included in the e-book have a model specifically designed for legal matters or high-level business negotiations which will provide greater levels of security. All of these tools have documentation that include a terms of service agreement. Be sure to review the terms of service to determine their security levels and whether they are sufficient for your purposes.

CHAPTER 3

CREATING A VIRTUAL LAW OFFICE

1. CONSUMER DEMAND FOR ONLINE LEGAL SERVICES

As you begin researching available virtual law practice options, you'll be reading articles that include words and concepts you have no comprehension of: Saas, Iaas, Paas (software as a service; infrastructure as a service; platform as a service), public clouds, private clouds, virtualization. Mind starts spinning, eyes glaze over, and soon those well-known desktop applications and fax machines seem like old, comfortable friends.

I understand. When I began the same search, the whole concept seemed very simple. I understood that SaaS systems were basically software packages that resided online rather than on your desktop. I analogized them to using Gmail, a web-based email service, rather than Microsoft Outlook, a desktop program. I was very naïve.

Being someone who likes accessing my email online no matter where I am, I became a raving fan of VLO technology. So I researched a variety of Saas law-practice platforms to determine what functionality each offered. I learned that you had options as to what components of your practice you could "take online," ranging from practice management, time management, billing/invoicing, document storage and case management, client contact, and document assembly to varied combinations of these functions, and finally to a fully functional virtual law office which clients could access through a client portal on your website. All of these systems were secured by bank-level security standards.

Today, this level of knowledge seems rudimentary, partly because I hadn't researched services other than Saas, and partly because the innovative uses of network and cloud infrastructure have given birth to a vast array of virtual choices. Enterprise systems, on-demand scalable data platforms, desktop virtualization, and other developments are quickly gaining ground as IT professionals scramble to create the most flexible cloud platforms to meet the explosion of responses to the varied demands of business, including larger law firms. However, although we will be talking about a variety of cloud systems, Saas is the optimal model for solos and small firms.

The demand for cost-effective, online legal services is surging with the number of people using the internet to transact business. The clear trend is toward e-commerce transactions. Consumers shop, bank, conduct business, and pay their credit cards and taxes online. According to a Forrester study, US online retail reached $175 billion in 2007 and is projected to grow to $335 billion by 2012. People expect to be able to do business online, and law clients expect to be able to connect with their lawyer there as well. In ABA's GP-Solo Division's Technology eReport, Richard Granat states:

> *A recent survey of more than 2,000 online users revealed that a majority of consumers expect good law firms to offer their services online in the next couple of years. The online poll revealed that nearly half (47%) of consumers would be more likely to choose a law firm that offered the convenience of online access to legal services and documents over one that had no online service capability. Some 56 percent said they expected good law firms to give customers the ability to use their services online in the next couple of years. Over two-fifths (43%) agreed that they would change law firms if an alternative firm offered a reduced fee in return for the consumer providing initial details about their matter online.*

In addition, it is estimated that 80 percent of those needing legal representation in the US do not receive it due to cost. This has raised a significant access to justice issue, and judges are alarmed at the increasing number of pro se litigants who cannot adequately represent themselves. Cloud technology, document assembly systems, and unbundling legal services enables us to render them affordable.

2. A LITTLE HISTORY

Interestingly, virtual law office technology was first employed to create web-based environments where individual attorneys in different locations could practice as a virtual firm. Wikipedia defines a virtual law office this way:

> *The term "virtual law firm" originally was used to refer to a group of lawyers with diverse expertise that are banded together through technological means to provide a suite of services to its clients. The first recorded virtual law firm was "Woolley & Co" set up in 1996 in England by Andrew Woolley. The term became better used from 2004. Virtual law firms are also often referred to as "Law Firm 2.0". The concept has now spread globally and is finding favour with clients seeking better service and value.*

> *According to earlier sources, a virtual law firm shared the following characteristics:*

> *Has a stable core group of attorneys;*

> *Has established collaborative relationships with other, specialized law firms that possess expertise that's occasionally needed;*

> *Is glued together with appropriate computer and telecommunications technology; and,*

> *Expands and reduces personnel as needed.*

These core characteristics are still mainly true seven years later, although the technology available to law firms has vastly expanded and improved. Just as web 2.0 has made sharing and online interaction almost commonplace, practice management software, including collaborative workspaces, has streamlined virtual interaction for lawyers, clients, and opposing parties in secure environments. The expanded and varied use of cloud computing has also made it far easier for companies to save and manage data across geographic locations securely and efficiently.

Nor has this model of virtual law practice gone by the wayside. For example, the British Columbia firm, Valkyrie Law Group, is entirely virtual. "There is no downtown Vancouver office with plush furniture and glamorous art in the reception. There are no assistants, no paralegal, no corporate services department and no law library."

3. WHAT IS CLOUD COMPUTING?

From a technology perspective, cloud computing has been defined by Jeff Kaplan from www.ThinkStrategies.com as: "a set of raw materials that users can put together to create optimal systems to meet objectives." It makes sense, but is not helpful to the layperson who can't wrap his or her mind around the whole where-is-my-stuff-on-the-internet experience. So let's take a look at it from a layperson's perspective.

The term "cloud computing" is really a misnomer and has nothing to do with clouds at all. In the American Bar Association's eLawyering task force paper called "Cloud Computing in Law Practice Management," attorney, author, and VLO developer Stephanie Kimbro describes the term's origin:

> *Law office data if hosted in the cloud is not actually floating around in an unknown location. Unfortunately, the term "in the cloud" tends to carry with it a sense of the unknown which is not an accurate description of the secure storage and transfer of electronic data ...*

> *The term "cloud computing" originates from the explanation that programmers used to describe complex networks and how the data was transferred from network to network. The space in which that data transferred from one law office's computer network was drawn in diagrams as a cloud to show that this information was now outside the control of the organization. This cloud is actually a known road and location that the data travels to and on and does not mean that the data is floating out in space unprotected and unobtainable.*

In reality, the information accessible online is stored on large servers located in data centers, much like desktop data is stored on local drives or in-house servers. The differences are scale, location, and accessibility. These servers, often called server farms, have massive storage capacity and can be located anywhere. Additionally, companies who own the servers often share capacity when their demand exceeds or drops below their existing capacity.

For lawyers, however, using web applications such as Google Apps for document storage or gmail for communication and document collaboration create jurisdictional, ethical, and security issues. This is why virtual law platforms must be developed with security levels specifically designed to meet the requirements of lawyers' ethical obligations to protect a client's privacy and confidentiality as well as jurisdictional and other ethical concerns.

4. IAAS AND PAAS PLATFORMS

The terms Iaas (infrastructure as a service) and Paas (platform as a service) refer to how storage ability is delivered. The "as a service" concept refers to the user's ability to call up the needed information on demand. The difference between these services is the degree to which your IT is involved in designing and implementing them.

Often referred to as enterprise systems, Iaas and Paas platforms are used by large corporations and law firms who have dedicated IT departments that work with service providers to design applications customized to the needs of the users. Iaas and Paas platforms are scalable and on-demand virtualized resources, which allows enterprise IT users to expand or reduce the amount of space as necessary. These systems are most beneficial to large, multi-office, or international firms that have complex communication and document security and retention needs, and need to have their systems custom-designed by their IT departments. For those interested in learning more, I suggest these two informative sites: HP Enterprise Technology and www.Appistry.com.

Big law has joined the international corporate community in voraciously adopting these cloud platforms, perhaps because they, like the corporate world, function nationwide or internationally, and have both the need and the capacity to change. They are far ahead of solos and small law firms, who appear to be out of their comfort zone with virtual practice models.

Given the numerous benefits of adopting VLO technology—one of which is that it levels the playing field with big law—solos and small law must move beyond these restraints to compete and survive by attracting clients in the existing legal marketplace who expect to be able to transact online.

5. THE SAAS MODEL

In addition to the development of law practice platforms on which law firm IT departments design and implement large-scale, customized law practice management systems, leading Saas vendors are increasingly designing their solutions to meet a growing number of specific business concerns. To that end, they have created pre-packaged applications delivered as an online service and designed to meet the specific needs of the legal industry. The drawback is that you don't get to design your own program; but a review of the Saas components reveals that developers willingly respond to input from users in their designs.

Simply put, Saas VLOs and practice management systems are fully designed, fully functional programs that live online rather than on your desktop. Each provider is unique in the services it offers and in how its service functions. There are no purchase costs, but you pay a monthly service fee, depending on the functionality. Some are strictly practice management tools that can be accessed through your web browser (a partial online law practice). Others are full-service law firms which include the capacity to communicate and interact with clients through a secured portal on your website (a true VLO as defined by the ABA's eLawyering Task Force). Still others include document assembly services combined with legal advice.

Thus, in choosing virtual services, the first thing you must think about is whether you want to take all, or just part, of your practice online.

Saas programs are generally easier to use and more intuitive than desktop software, and require no updates or maintenance by the user. Looked at in another way, you are basically outsourcing to the vendor all the work associated with the installation, information migration, maintenance, malfunction issues, and upgrades. The benefits of Saas VLOs are:

- The advantages of an "enterprise" system without the burden of getting it up and running or paying for maintenance, upgrades, or support
- The ability to provide service to the "latent market for legal services" who do not seek alternatives to legal assistance through online document assembly sites
- The advantage of the vendor's latest technological features without the disruptions to service and costs associated with software upgrades

- The ability to provide services throughout the entire state in which you are licensed
- No up-front capital investment
- Greater productivity at a lower cost of ownership
- Greater flexibility and scalability (enlarge/reduce) to meet changing business requirements
- No installation or configuration time lag
- No need for brick and mortar office space (reduced overhead)
- Enables you to practice wherever you have an internet connection (secured, of course)
- Communicate and collaborate with clients, other lawyers, or anyone associated with your work anywhere, at any time
- Expand a client base through the reach and visibility of an online presence
- Meet client demands for delivery of legal services online
- Allows clients to feel more "in control" of the legal matter by giving them 24/7 access to their documents, correspondence, and email
- Invoice and accept payments online
- Intuitive and comprehensive case management functionality
- Provide online legal advice and document review
- Create searchable and linkable legal library for clients
- Ability to counsel pro se clients
- Provide pro bono services online

As previously mentioned, each Saas vendor provides its own unique functionality with respect to the design of the application it offers. Some of the variations are:

- Full law practice management functions
- Full law practice management functions, including securitized client communication and collaboration
- Full law practice management and communication accessed seamlessly through your website portal
- Full law practice management and communication accessed through your website portal, including document assembly options
- Case management functions, not including global office functions or document management
- Document management systems and storage
- Calendaring, time tracking, and invoicing
- Contact management

VLOs designed to function as full office automation include the following functions:

- Client access to data and communication through a fully securitized website portal
- May or may not include document assembly
- Jurisdiction checks
- Conflicts of interest checks
- Online engagement/creation of attorney/client relationship
- Client data intake
- Contact management
- Billing and online invoice management and implementation
- Calendaring

- Document storage
- Direct, secured client communication through internal email functions with document attachment capabilities
- Law and research libraries
- On-line bill payment
- Trust accounting

Richard Granat, co-chair of the ABA's eLawyering Task Force, and owner of DirectLaw.com, describes fully functional VLOs in this way:

A law firm web site that is based on eLawyering concept involves moving beyond a law firm web site that contains only legal content to one that helps clients collaborate with their lawyer and do legal tasks over the Internet. The impact of these web based, interactive applications is to save lawyer time, and often increase lawyer productivity and profit margins, while providing a more satisfying experience for the client …. For these law firms, the web site becomes the primary way in which the law firm relates to its clients and manages the flow of legal work.

He explains the reasoning behind the definition of a virtual law office:

When we started the eLawyering Task Force in 2000 our focus, then and now, is the delivery of online legal services. By online legal services we envisioned the combination of digital applications integrated with the services of a lawyer. A good example of this would be web-enabled document automation, where the client completes an online questionnaire which instantly creates the first draft of a document ready for the lawyers review, further advice, and amendment, producing a final document ready for filing or execution. We believe that implementation of models like this results in higher law firm productivity and profitability, resulting sometimes in lower fees. I can think of many other digital applications like web-enabled document automation which fit into this category.

In 2003 I launched a law firm model in Maryland where I am a member of the bar at http://www.mdfamilylawyer.com and called in a "virtual law firm" as an example of elawyering concepts.

In order to implement elawyering applications for clients online, what is called a "persistent session" has to be created online, where a user can save answers and information to a data base or other application. So for example, to use the document automation example again, answers can be saved, and the user can return to the questionnaire multiple times. Moreover, to make the site ethically compliant, the user has to accept a "Limited Retainer Services Agreement." Other functions such as a customized calendar for the client, the storage of the client's documents online, online legal advice functions, all require a secure connection and a place where this personalized information *can be saved securely and accessible only by the client.*

Technically the only way to do this is to have a secure client space which can be logged on only with that client's username and password. We call that web architecture a "client portal."

We also developed a set of guidelines for law firms delivering legal services online that dealt with, in part, with the concepts of security of client data and client communications. See generally, http://www.elawyering.com

According to the same ABA Technology Study, 98% of lawyers now use email to communicate with their clients. I don't doubt that a reasonable percentage, say 20%, never see a client in their office and communicate with them only by email. In a sense these law firms are operating in a total virtual environment, but it is not helpful in terms of advancing the state of the art to simply characterize all of these law firms as "virtual law firms." Instead we thought it would be useful and important to develop some criteria about what a "virtual law firm" is, and criteria for offering legal services online, not only so that consumers have confidence in dealing with lawyers online, but also in terms of how to think about innovation when lawyers deliver legal services over the web.

Of course, technology evolves faster than we can write about it, and practice management systems and collaborative workspaces have been developed incorporating many of the features that may constitute a VLO under the eLawyering task force's guidelines. For example, Clio is a practice management system that offers an internal client contact system to enable secured communication and the ability to collaborate on document preparation. PBWorks is a collaborative environment that enables the creation of any kind of workspace you might want, including case and matter management, client extranet, legal research database, co-counsel relationships, and deal rooms. MyRealPractice offers the uniqueness of combining practice management with marketing management and automated suggestions and reminders.

Saas systems are a perfect fit for the nature of solo and small firm practices. The variety of applications available as virtual law practice tools requires that you take the time to review them in order to determine how you would like your practice to function. There is also developing capability for different services to integrate their functions, allowing you to custom-design the functionality of your system. For example, Advologix, a Saas law practice management system built on the Salesforce platform, has recently collaborated with NetDocuments, a powerful document management and storage system, to create a high-level management system that is capable of storing, categorizing, and searching large numbers of documents.

Before beginning your research, make a list of the things you want the software to do. Consider the following:

- Do you want to offer unbundled legal services, offer full-service representation, or both?

- Do you want to be able to communicate directly with your client online?
- Will you be collaborating with other attorneys or creating a multi-jurisdictional virtual firm through your VLO?
- What specific tasks do you want your VLO to automate?

Use that as a starting point; your list will most certainly change once you've had the chance to review your options. I have included a list of virtual law firm platforms in the e-book. Take the time to visit the websites, review their online demos, and request one-to-one phone consultations to help you walk through how these sites work. Also keep in mind that the variations allow you to be creative in integrating your use of these applications into your practice.

6. DOCUMENT ASSEMBLY FUNCTIONS AND UNBUNDLING LEGAL SERVICES

If you spend time investigating VLO platforms, you will come across some that offer document assembly functions, the use of which is often referred to as unbundling legal services. Document assembly has acquired something of a bad reputation. The concept was first introduced by non-lawyer businesses like LegalZoom, which, like other non-lawyer corporations, offer packaged documents without the added (and necessary) legal advice with regard to completing the documents, or making appropriate changes depending on the client's circumstances.

The ABA Standing Committee on the Delivery of Legal Services issued a 2009 white paper entitled "An Analysis of Rules that Allow Lawyers to Serve Pro Se Litigants," in which it concluded that offering unbundled services, or limited legal representation, could benefit both the pro se litigants and the court system, as the market for document preparation and limited advocacy grows. In a post entitled "The Truth about Unbundled Legal Services," Total Attorneys reported:

The key to making sound decisions about unbundled legal services is a solid understanding of exactly what unbundled legal services are and are not. For the attorney, that means thoroughly reviewing state and local bar association opinions on the ethical delivery of unbundled services. 28 states and one local bar association have issued ethics opinions on the unbundling of legal services; information about current ethical rules in many states is available through the Committee'sPro Se/Unbundling Resource Center. It also means understanding the apparently competing products on the market and how they truly differ from the services offered by a virtual law firm. Finally, the attorney must prepare materials and information to make the extent and limitations of the service clear to the prospective client, and to ensure that prospects understand the difference between unbundled legal services provided by an attorney and legal document preparation services or DIY providers.

However, as technology moves more legal functions toward the commodity side of Susskind's categorization, companies like LegalZoom are proliferating. The UK, in passing the Legal Services Act of 2007 (aka the "Tesco Law") has gone even further by including authorization of Alternative Business Structures (ABS), allowing lawyers and non-lawyers to partner or invest capital in establishing a law firm or legal services provider. These entities insure the move toward standardized or systematized legal functions and create a significant threat to the structure of law practice as we know it. **This very real possibility makes it all the more imperative that lawyers adopt more service-model systems into their practice to compete with businesses eyeing legal services delivery as a significant income source**.

The VLOs that offer document assembly functions are different in that they can be used in conjunction with limited legal representation (thus the name unbundled legal services). Document assembly functions can be offered as one of many ways clients can use your services.

Because many prospective clients do not understand the difference between a VLO providing unbundled legal services and a document preparation service such as LegalZoom, they may question why your document assembly services are more costly. Make sure that your prospects and clients understand what they're getting for their money; specifically, that you offer document preparation combined with the necessary legal knowledge and professional judgment that non-lawyer providers cannot give them.

Document automation works through the use of client questionnaires designed to complete the variables within a pre-drafted document, such as a will or trust, a particular kind of contact, business formation, etc. The clients' responses to the questions then automatically complete the variables in the document. However, upon review, you may find that their responses require additional investigation into their intent or objectives, which can result in revisions to the pre-drafted document. In these instances, your legal advice and recommendations are required so that the document accomplishes its desired result and keeps the client out of trouble.

7. PERMANENT CHANGE OR PASSING PHASE?

As the Eversheds Report referred to in Chapter 1 makes clear, the dynamics at play have created a permanent change in the way we practice. The processes of practicing law in this new environment have resulted from clients demands, and a shift to a client-centric focus. This represents not just a change in process, but also a change in motivation. By becoming a client-centric lawyer, you are not just transforming how you do things, but also why, because you must put the needs of your clients ahead of your own. That represents a philosophical shift in your thinking if your original plan was to get rich by becoming a professional.

In her blog post "The Future of the Legal Profession is Client-Centric," Stephanie Kimbro puts it like this:

Through the use of technology and especially through the security of virtual law practice we have much more effective communication with our clients. Why would we as attorneys want to give that up either? …. The benefit should be that the use of technology gives us the ability to better serve our clients and the time to focus on actually solving problems for individuals rather than getting bogged down in administrative tasks that we later have to find ways to cover in our legal fees …. While many trends in business are cyclical, it is hard to imagine that any attorney or law firm would survive for long trying to go back to providing less customer service to their clients. So in effect, these changes that we see occurring in our profession, partly because they are client-centric, are not going anywhere.

No one is saying the road less traveled is without risk. Innovation always creates new opportunities, but those untested opportunities always carry with them the risk of unintended consequences. The point, however, is that if you want to practice law, and you want to be able to survive in a market made more competitive by developing innovative technology-based legal delivery models, you have no choice but to embrace these trends.

CHAPTER 4

SECURITY, ETHICS, AND REGULATION IN THE CLOUD

The use of cloud technology in a law practice is not without its challenges, and many of you may be aware of emerging state bar opinions containing guidelines and regulations related to a virtual practice. The American Bar Association has also now taken an aggressive interest in catching up with the integration of this technology into the practice. The market push toward the cloud, the security risks and ethical considerations for lawyers, and the attempts to regulate this essentially new law practice model have converged, and now there is a struggle to put reasonable standards in place that will not have a chilling effect on the expansion of virtual-based law firms.

To that end, the ABA's Law Practice Management Section created the eLawyering Task Force and the Ethics 2020 Commission to guide the evolutionary process. The eLawyering Task Force issued guidelines entitled "Suggested Minimum Requirements for Law Firms Delivering Legal Services Online." The focus of the Ethics 2020 Commission is to investigate whether the virtual practice of law is compliant with the Model Rules, or whether further regulation is advisable and/or necessary. They have issued the ABA Commission on Ethics 20/20 Preliminary Issues Outline, and reviewed comments on Dec. 15, 2010. Their final opinion will be issued in the near future, hopefully incorporating the concerns raised by those who commented on the outline. Both the Suggested Minimum Requirements and Issues Outline should be reviewed for a thorough understanding of the security and ethical issues that must be addressed.

1. SECURITY

We previously discussed the marketplace demand for online services and the benefits to the practice of using cloud technology. If it is now legal to purchase legal documents from supermarket kiosks in the UK, Wales, and now Scotland, it's not too much of a stretch that at a minimum, document assembly services will be one of several methods of delivering legal services to clients that the majority of law firms large and small will offer very soon.

With all of the concern about security and privacy, it is amazing that so many lawyers rely on Google Apps or Microsoft Live to communicate and store or disseminate documents. For years, lawyers have been communicating with their clients, and creating and transmitting documents, via open source platforms (e.g., Google docs).It is clear that using these unsecured platforms to communicate with clients and share documents is fraught with legal pitfalls. While both Google and Microsoft have taken some steps to securitize their data, their efforts are far from sufficient to meet the standards lawyers must adhere to.

For example, Google has made encryption available to Gmail users, but only in the paid premier application (the cost is minimal at $50/year) and only if you specifically request it. Moreover, your emails are not encrypted end-to-end unless the person you are emailing has also encrypted his or her emails on that end. Likewise, you can request that documents be encrypted, but Google only encrypts them during transmission, not storage. The data that is not properly secured creates confidentiality and attorney/client privilege issues.

On the other hand, if you are using a virtual platform designed for law office use that includes a communication function, both you and your client communicate directly through a bank-level secured, encrypted email system, and documents are stored in the same level of security.

In order to ensure that these safeguards are in place, it is necessary to do due diligence regarding the VLO or cloud vendor to determine, among other things, what security measures they employ, where their data centers are located, and how they are protected. You need to determine their data retention policies and clarify what process will be employed to return data in response to a discovery request or if the company goes out of business. If the hosting company contracts with third-party server companies, you need to know the terms of their agreement to be sure third parties are required to adhere to the guidelines necessary to protect legal data. Jack Newton, President of Clio, a Saas practice management product, has described in detail the security issues you should be concerned with in his article "Saas Security: Can You Trust Your Data in the Cloud?"

When researching these providers, be sure to ask:
- Where are the primary servers located?
- Where are the servers located that back up the data?
- How often, and in what manner, is users' data backed up?
- What are the jurisdiction's regulatory require-ments? (More about why location is an issue to follow)
- Do they engage in cross-border data transfers? If so, when and where? Will you be notified? Is there a compliance plan for cross-border transfers?
- Do they employ tier 4, 256-bit encryption, bank-level security?
- Are these security measures in place both while the data is in transition and in storage?
- Have their operations ever been audited? (If so, obtain a copy of the report)
- Do they own their servers, or lease them from a third party?
- If they do not own them, what are the terms of the third-party agreement? (Obtain a copy)
- Will your data be stored on a dedicated server, or on a multi-tenancy server? (i.e., with others' data)
- If multi-tenant, how is your data segregated from others'?
- How is the server building physically secured?
- Who has access to the stored data?
- What kind of training do their employees undergo?

- Have they ever had a security breach?
- What is their customer notification policy upon breach?
- What is their response policy upon breach?
- What is their disaster recovery/business continuity plan?
- What is their protocol concerning access to and exportation of your data?
- What is their history—e.g., how long have they been in business, and where do they derive their funding?
- Are they Safe-Harbor certified? (Insures that their security measures comply with the EU Directive, a comprehensive regulatory scheme. Not necessary, but comfortable)

Always be sure to back up your data on your own hard drive to mitigate any loss of data that may occur if you lose your internet connection, or if there is any unrecovered data loss due to a vendor downtime.

2. ETHICAL CONSIDERATIONS

Practicing law via a cloud technology raises questions as to how you meet your ethical obligations to your clients. In "Guest Post: Ethics Considerations for the Virtual Practice of Law," Stephanie Kimbro makes the following observation:

> *The delivery of legal services online carries with it a number of ethical concerns; however, these ethical concerns are not all that unlike those that have traditionally been addressed by offline law firms. The online lawyer is able*

to mitigate risks associated with virtual law practice just as a traditionally-practicing attorney would with an offline practice when, for example, installing and using software for law practice management.

In other words, just as lawyers in traditional practice must take measures to safeguard their clients' files and meet other ethical obligations, so must cloud-based lawyers concern themselves with best practices in insuring the same level of diligence. Here are several areas of concern with respect to those obligations:

- **Identity & Residency**: Because your communications with potential clients may be conducted solely online, you need to take all necessary steps to carefully establish the identity and residency of the person or entity seeking your representation to avoid unauthorized practice of law.

- **Creation of the Attorney/Client Relationship**: You must establish and clearly state the point at which the attorney/client relationship is created, as online communications will occur before a formal relationship is established. This can be done through the use of a click-wrap agreement, which typically explains the conditions of the attorney's representation, the nature of unbundled legal services, and defines the scope of representation.

- **Define the Scope of Representation**: You must clearly define the scope of representation, which may lack clarity even in traditional practice. In a practice involving unbundled services or limited representation, there are always certain items that are outside the attorney's responsibility and scope of agreement. Be sure mutual obligations are adequately defined in writing.

- **Take Security Measures**: Insure confidentiality of client data by performing the duties outlined in the security section above.
- **Conflict of Interest:** Run both online and offline conflict checks.
- **Competency:** Be sure that the kind of legal matter presented by your client can be adequately handled through virtual law office technology. If it cannot, consider what parts could be, and integrate them with traditional lawyering practices such as meeting face to face, etc.
- **Conflict of Laws:** If the matter you are considering handling is in federal court, but requires filing an action in a state court you are not licensed to practice in, you should not represent that client in either matter.
- **Educate Yourself:** Stay current on security issues and best practices for the use of mobile devices.
- **Educate Your Client:** Make your client aware of the steps you are taking to protect his or her data and confidentiality, and advise him or her to do the same (i.e., don't post about the legal matter on Facebook).

There are those who may feel uncomfortable interacting with their clients only via email. The answer to that problem is simple: expand your interaction to telephone calls or in-person meetings if you or the client finds those interactions necessary or beneficial. There are no restrictions here, only opportunities to engage in various methods of representation not otherwise available; and at a minimal cost with the utmost convenience.

For an in-depth look at these issues, InformationLaw-Group.com ran a 15-part series called The Legal Implications of Cloud Computing. It is very much worth your while to read through the series, which gives a thorough analysis of the evolution of legal issues and regulatory responses concerning the cloud. Other sources of current information are Stephanie Kimbro's VirtualLawPractice.org, the ABA LPM's eLawyering Task Force and the ABA's Ethics 2020 Commission.

Think creatively: Using VLO technology allows you to create a law practice with almost no start-up costs and to continue to function with very little overhead. Once you are able to generate income, you might find that you want to combine your practice with a traditional brick and mortar office practice, and that is very easily done. Again, your options in creating a practice style that suits you are only enhanced by the technology available.

In addition, having a virtual presence through both content marketing and your practice solidifies your brand as a tech-savvy lawyer readily available to a growing community of web users who expect to capitalize on the convenience of online transactions.

3. REGULATION OF SECURITY STANDARDS AND ETHICAL OBLIGATIONS

As previously mentioned, while there is increasing movement toward cloud adoption in the practice of law, there is also concern among regulatory bodies that the use of this technology be regulated in accordance with existing ethical obligations. However, it is now being seen that the existing rules of professional conduct were not drafted in alignment with the circumstances now presented by the use of modern technology. Different countries have taken different approaches to this concern.

The European Union has comprehensive security regulations called the EU Data Protection Directive, which was drafted to both encourage and facilitate the use of evolving cloud technology, but also to provide reasonable and sensible regulation of its use. Each member state implements the directive via its own regulation, creating yet another layer of variation among nations. Most notably, one of the critical terms of the directive is that it *prohibits* the transfer of personal information from the EU to any country that does not provide adequate levels of data protection, which includes the US.

In contrast, the United States has approached security regulation and standards from a piecemeal perspective, instituting regulation as specific concerns arise. Existing regulations include:

- **The Sarbanes-Oxley Act**—requires public companies to comply with email retention, data security and oversight requirements
- **Payment Card Industry Data Security Standard (PCI-DSS)**—requires enhancement of payment account data security
- **Health Insurance Portability and Accountability Act (HIPAA)**—regulates use and disclosure of health information
- **Federal Information Security Management Act (FISMA)**—requires federal agencies to develop and implement information security programs related to their own operations

- **COPPA**—regulates online data collection of children under thirteen
- **The Gramm-Leach-Bliley Act**—regulates disclosure of non-public information by financial institutions

Individual US states have also instituted regulations and standards that must be considered in choosing data location. In a recent webinar presented by Sandra Jaskie and Jonathan Armstrong of Duane Morris, LLP, the presenters noted that Massachusetts and Nebraska passed legislation requiring encryption of personal information and imposing responsibilities on vendors related to notice of data breach. Massachusetts also requires development of a security and privacy plan for all personal data that is either in storage or transmission on *any* (read mobile) device, and imposes stiff penalties for non-compliance.

In an attempt to bridge these different privacy approaches and provide a streamlined means for US organizations to comply with the European Directive, the US Department of Commerce and the European Commission developed a "Safe Harbor" certification process. The process enables individual US vendors to self-certify compliance with the EU directive, thereby eliminating the data transfer restriction. There is also a US–Swiss Safe Harbor Framework, since Switzerland is non-EU member state.

For US vendors whose servers reside in the US and who do not target European markets, Safe Harbor certification is not necessary, but sets standards that US vendors should strive to meet. But for document storage vendors whose systems also provide for online collaboration, certification is necessary due to the high rate of international collaboration among businesses and law firms.

InfosecIsland.com's blog entitled "Cloud Computing Data Protection World Map" includes a link to a great visual, coded to show worldwide security protection levels.

4. THE FUTURE OF INTERNATIONAL SECURITY REGULATION

The economic viability of conducting business online—including the business of law—is the significant driver in this scenario. If the continued economic instability of global financial markets has taught us anything, it is that cost-efficiency will be of enduring prominence. Because cost-efficiency is the trademark of cloud computing and virtualization, there is no doubt that international cooperation will improve. In fact, it is already moving in that direction.

Duane Morris recently reported that:
- The UK's Information Commissioner's Office (ICO) issued its new Code of Practice on handling personal information online
- A new EU directive is likely within the next two years
- There are moves at harmonization, both within Europe and with the US, with EU data-privacy regulators holding a meeting with the FTC

Project Counsel discussed several sources of potential for global security regulation:

- the European Commission and the US have opened negotiations on the creation of a data protection agreement to govern data transfers between the EU and the US
- In Washington, Viviane Reding, Commissioner for Justice, Fundamental Rights and Citizenship, made clear her agenda to begin negotiations with the US on an umbrella data protection agreement
- The European Parliament gave approval to the latest framework within which US authorities can gain access to Europeans' banking details to aid counter-terrorism intelligence

These security and ethical matters may seem burdensome, and appear to outweigh the benefits and efficiency of using cloud technology to run your practice. But consider this: in five years, you won't have a choice. I recently attended the College of Law Practice Management's 2010 Futures Conference and can say without hesitation that the bell signaling the end of lawyering as we know it is ringing loud and clear. Recently, Thomson Reuters, the world's largest legal publisher servicing lawyers and law firms, purchased Pangea3, a major LPO player in India. This purchase has the potential of changing Thomson Reuters to a competitor rather than a service provider. With 55,000 employees and offices worldwide, Thomson Reuters' Pangea3 could soon become the number one provider of legal services to consumers, if that is their intention.

Staying competitive in this environment requires that you make the leap sooner or later. As Stephanie Kimbro states in her blog post, "The Future of Law Practice is Client-Centric," "your clients are all online, and you need to be there, too."

CHAPTER 5:

CONTENT MARKETING, PART 1

1. CONTENT VS. SOCIAL MEDIA MARKETING

Most people would call what we're going to talk about here "social media marketing." But I think social media marketing is something different than the kind of online strategies lawyers should use to get themselves in front of their target client base. Why? Because this strategy is not aimed at selling products to consumers; it's aimed at providing information in a way that will attract your target clients to you, creating the opportunity for conversation, engagement, and representation. There's nothing wrong with using social media marketing strategies to sell products, but that's not what we're doing here.

Yes, the process is similar, the tools are the same, but the content is different. We're using keywords and tags and metadata to entice the search engines, but within a context that provides value to our target clients. The information needs to be useful, accurate, and reliable.

In a blog post on www.Webinknow.com called "Brand Journalism", David Meerman Scott, marketer, speaker, author, and thought leader on social media marketing trends, defines the difference like this:

> *Brand Journalism is when any organization— B2B company, consumer product company, the military, nonprofits, government agencies, politicians, churches, rock bands, solo entrepreneurs—creates valuable information and shares it with the world.*

> *Brand Journalism is not a product pitch. It is not an advertorial. It is not an egotistical spewing of gobbledygook-laden corporate drivel.*

> *Instead Brand Journalism is the creation of Web content—videos, blog posts, photos, charts, graphs, essays, ebooks, white papers—that delivers value to your marketplace and serves to position your organization as one worthy of doing business with.*

Our market is the 80 percent of potential clients in the US who cannot afford high hourly billing, but are in need of answers to their problems online. They are not consumers looking for a deal on a pair of shoes. They Google for the "how to's" rather than the "where can I find's." And when your market finds information about a legal issue on your website and then learns that you offer easy accessibility and alternative fee arrangements, chances are the conversation will begin.

Ruth M. Shipley recently reviewed the book *Crush It: Why Now is the Time to Cash In on Your Passion* by Gary

Vaynerchuk on www.SocialMediaExaminer.com. Gary is the famed wine seller and social media marketer. *Crush It* is the story of how he took a $2 million wine business and turned it into a $20 million business using social media. Ruth says:

> **Crush It! will give you the techniques you need to establish your expertise using social media. Vaynerchuk calls it "building your personal brand." Here are the techniques in a nutshell:**
> - *Identify your passion.*
> - *Learn as much about it as you can.*
> - *Start blogging about it.*
> - *Find other blogs about it and leave comments.*
> - *Find Facebook pages about your passion, become a friend/fan and contribute.*
> - *Search Twitter to find other passionate people and talk to them.*
> - *Repeat steps 2 through 6 over and over and over.*

That was his strategy. And while that may seem like an oversimplification of what goes into this process, notice this: his top two steps were to identify his passion, and learn as much as he could about it. Then he started talking. And when he started talking, everybody listened. Because by educating himself ("learn as much about it as you can"), he provided valuable information and created a strong personal brand, an online presence that reached out and engaged the social media community.

Content marketing is more subtle than Gary Vaynerchuk's style (which I find delightful, but not necessarily appropriate for lawyers). Wine consumers are not looking for a treatise on how a certain kind of grape will affect their digestive system (or maybe they are?). On the other hand, the people we are reaching out to are not consumers, although they are sometimes described that way in a business context. They are people in need of help. They want to know how their lives will be affected by something that is occurring, something they are doing, something that can change the direction of their lives. This is simply a very different crowd than the consumer society.

At first glance, content marketing makes no sense. If you are giving all your information away for free, why would anyone pay for your services?

Jay Fleischman, a New York attorney who has built a successful practice around content marketing, puts it like this:

> *The social media intelligentsia will tell you that by putting content out there and making it free, you become invested with social capital. People look to you are the de facto expert, and they'll flock to your law firm when they need your help. What they don't explain is why anyone with half a brain would hire you once you tell them everything you know. They merely assure you it's the case.*

> *Maybe some of your potential clients will try to use your law firm content marketing efforts to do some of the legwork, and that's fine. But when push comes to shove and the big deal issues present themselves, the clients are going to call you.*

Because what you do is not merely technical, it's infused with years of experience. Knowledge of your judges and trustees doesn't translate effectively into content. You can't replicate finesse and analysis of difficult scenarios.

Here are Jay's top 11 reasons why online legal marketing efforts must be centered around the creation of real content instead of marketing fluff:

1. <u>Content informs people </u>*about the basics before they pick up the phone to call you for an initial meeting;*

2. *Your online legal marketing efforts need to be designed to prove that your law firm is well-educated in solving client needs, and can communicate those solutions effectively;*

3. *When you show how much you know, you don't need to tell your prospective clients about your competence—the proof is in the pudding;*

4. *Informative content gets passed along from one person to the next, providing exposure to more people than would otherwise be possible using other marketing techniques;*

5. *When your law firm creates useful content—not fluff—it helps you learn more about it even if you've been practicing law for years;*

6. *Valuable content allows your online legal marketing efforts to weed out those people who do not need your help—someone reads your stuff, they realize the solution you offer isn't for them, and they move on without wasting your time or theirs;*

7. *Providing information as the basis of your marketing efforts gives people the ability to do some*

of the "grunt work" that you'd like them to do before meeting with you. Stuff like writing a letter to a debt collector to stop contacting them, initiating an effective credit reporting reinvestigation request, or putting together all of the documents they'll need to start a bankruptcy case. Why would you not want them to do this legwork before coming to you in the first place?

8. *While you're marketing your law firm by providing valuable information, others are marketing with the bland and forgettable 30 second TV spot (and people are skipping it to hit the bathroom or grab a snack);*

9. *Creating a <u>blog post</u>, article or other form of content takes time but no money;*

10. *You can re-purpose your content by taking <u>blog posts</u> and turning them into an <u>ebook or informational package</u> to provide to clients, so you can create it once and spin it out to use over and over again;*

11. *More content marketing = more search engine saturation = <u>higher placement on the search engines</u> = more traffic to your website or blog = more clients = **more money**.*

2. HOW CONTENT AND SOCIAL MEDIA MARKETING WORK (THE REALLY BASIC VERSION)

Let's take a look at what content marketing, or social media marketing, really is. In its most simple form, it is a system of marketing using web 2.0 tools to create or increase business. It costs nothing except your time in learning and developing the skills necessary to use the system effectively. It has become the marketing system of choice because it reaches clients and customers where they are: online. It does so by creating interaction, communication, and collaboration among online users, both colleagues and clients. It is comprised of user-generated content such as blogs, microblogs, and other forms of social media input.

For marketing purposes, the ultimate goal of this activity is to create a community—your network—around a product or service that you offer. In that way, you've created an entire force of enthusiasts who will amplify your offerings to their friends and family, online and otherwise. These communities can be your email subscribers, Facebook friends, Twitter followers, LinkedIn connections, and members of other social network sites. In this way, your presence, content, and product or service "go viral," which basically means it gets spread around other online communities, reaching more and more potential clients or consumers who are online searching for goods and services.

Back in the day (1990s–2000s), before web 2.0 evolved, online marketers focused exclusively on search engine optimization (SEO) for the major browsers such as Google (there were others, but who remembers them?). SEO is certainly still important, and you must always use SEO strategies in creating your online content—more about that later.

But there's a new strategy in town call social media optimization (SMO) which analyzes the use of web 2.0 tools to optimize your results. The two processes are very different: SEO focuses on keywords and tags associated with your content, which requires some research on your part to find out what the online user is searching for. SMO, on the other hand, requires research into the most relevant social platforms for placement of your content. It also analyzes the use of tools to make your content go viral, such as RSS feeds and sharing functions. It also requires what its name implies: being social.

In order to make effective use of SEO and SMO systems and tactics, however, you must have your own goals and strategies in order. Let's take a look at some of the things you must decide for yourself before beginning your marketing campaign:

- What is your passion?

Remember Gary Vaynerchuk's list? Absolutely very first question to answer. Why? Two reasons: first, because your passion will shine through your content and attract readers, who are in turn excited about your enthusiasm and want to know more about you and what you do; second, if you're not passionate about what you are doing, why are you doing it? It's easy to be dispassionate when you can hide it in a crowd of, say, the other 100 lawyers in your firm. But when you're out on the front lines of your own battlefield, a lack of passion about the services you offer is transparent, and will lead to failure every time.

- Who is your target client base?

What is the niche market your passion will serve? It can be much more specific than corporate law, or family law. How about a particular function of a large corporation? A specific kind of small business? Specific realignment or expansion of a business or corporation? You can do all of the above, but by defining the kinds of representation you perform precisely, you can base your marketing content on those activities. That gives you plenty of topics to blog about, and plenty of keywords to incorporate. By categorizing yourself simply as a corporate lawyer, however, you will get lost in the competition.

Getting these two steps right from the beginning is the most important thing you can do to build a solid foundation for your marketing system. Everything else you do must always meet the test of whether or not it supports your passion and serves your niche market and target client base.

Once that is accomplished, content marketing involves five steps:

1. Participating in social networking sites
2. Blogging
3. Syndicating your blog post on social network sites
4. Using subscription tools to create a following
5. Repurposing your content for ebooks, articles, white papers and videos

What does this process create? Listening, connecting, informing, a personal brand, conversation, community, all of the characteristics that make social media the most powerful marketing method in our culture today.

In a wonderful post entitled Social Media Delivers Law Firm.Content to the People Who Want It, Adrian Lurssen of JDSupra.com responds to a blog post that criticizes the use of social media for distribution of content. Not so, he says, citing the numerous incidences of those who subscribe to receive information:

The numbers tell a different story. Across our legal news channels, over 100,000 people have requested to receive legal updates, client alerts, articles, newsletters, blog posts and the like on all topics from our lawyers and law firms, often delivered to them on the major social networks... Our subscribers not only read the content, they also share it with their own networks of friends and colleagues. And, it is clear that, far from losing trust, this sharing of substantive content builds trust.

3. PARTICIPATING IN SOCIAL NETWORKING SITES

Before you launch your website, have your business cards printed, or take any action to launch your practice, you MUST start participating in social media and networking sites. Why? Because one of the primary objectives is to create conversation and relationship, and thisdoesn't happen in a day. How long it does take depends on your own commitment to learn how to use these tools and your comfort level in communicating with people you don't know (we will discuss this more when we talk about syndication). It also gives you immediate access to lots of information that you will find useful in creating your practice. By starting early, you can jump right in with your content contributions when you are ready.

An important point to keep in mind is that web 2.0 is a fluid, dynamic medium, which is why, although we will talk about particular sites, we must remember that they are not social media; rather, they are the tools that allow us to participate in social media. And they change. All the time. So participation is really being social online through whatever tools or sites are the most beneficial to you personally and professionally to accomplish the things we've discussed: listening, conversing, interacting, relating, giving, and taking.

For example, say you always use the same road when you drive to work in the morning. But say that road is getting too crowded, and they are now building a new one to accommodate the traffic. When they are finished, you start using the new road to go to work. Because your goal is not to use the road. Your goal is to get to work. Make sense?

We all know the three big networking sites: Twitter, Facebook, and LinkedIn. The intricacies of using the big three are beyond the scope of this book, but there is lots of help out there from social media marketers. Remember, however, that like blogging, there is a difference between using social networking sites to sell products online and using them to gain the confidence and trust of potential clients.

Although lawyers certainly represent a minority of users on them, they are absolutely essential to an *effective online presence*—a major component of a successful marketing campaign. These sites, along with others more profession-specific, represent the major sources of online interaction, other than personal email. This is where information is sought and found, business relationships are developed, business referrals are made, areas of expertise are showcased and found, opportunities are created, collaboration is established, and business ventures are found and launched.

These sites are so powerful because they can draw from local, state-wide, national, and international professional communities. The connectivity capabilities of web 2.0 enable us to grow relationships with anyone, anywhere. For practicing attorneys, it opens their potential client base up to the entire state or states in which they are licensed. For attorneys engaged in corporate, copyright, patent, cross-jurisdiction, and cyberlaw practices, content marketing can reach businesses around the globe.

Different sites serve different functions. *Twitter* is a source of constant engagement and interaction where people who "follow" each other share information that enables them to stay on the leading edge of whatever topics are of interest to them and create relationships through listening and responding. With the advent of pages within its structure, *Facebook* has moved from casual interaction to another way of capturing the online community as potential clients or customers. *LinkedIn* is primarily a source for professional networking, which lead to referrals and business opportunities. There are literally hundreds of ways to interweave the use of the big three sites to maximize exposure, but that is the subject of another book. Or two.

Law-specific sites I advise using are:
- **Martindale-Hubbell Connected**, a legal industry-only membership site much like LinkedIn,

but with the added advantage of internally-generated events on significant industry topics;

- **JDSupra**, a publisher of legal content ranging from court-filed documents to articles on substantive issues and law practice matters; and
- **myLegal.com**, a networking site for lawyers and legal service providers where critical information regarding services is acquired, and a potential client base can be developed
- If you're in-house, **LegalOnRamp.com** is the place to develop relationships, exchange ideas and information, and advance your brand

While these sites function differently, they serve common purposes:

- Sharing knowledge
- Showcasing content
- Networking and communicating
- Building relationships
- Developing thought leadership
- Engaging clients/customers
- Collaborating

Participating on these networks enlarges your online presence and lends credibility to your content marketing pieces, which you syndicate by publishing them on these sites. By interacting thoughtfully and consistently with the members of your social groups, you have given your friends, followers, or group members reason to read and refer your blog posts, articles, and other materials to the members of their social groups. This is how you get your content materials in front of your target clients, which link back to your website, creating traffic, subscribers, community, and clients.

A recent survey conducted by professional inbound marketing experts at www.Hubspot.com called "The State of Inbound Marketing 2010" supports the theory that these methods work. Here are the three key take-aways from the survey:

Inbound Marketing Channels Continue to Deliver Dramatically Lower Cost Per Lead than Outbound Channels Do. Businesses spending 50% or more of their marketing budget on Inbound Marketing activities spent 60% less per lead than businesses spending 50% or more of their marketing budget on outbound channels. This number is remarkably consistent with the 61% lower cost businesses reported a year ago. Clearly, inbound marketing channels are maintaining their low-cost advantage.

Social Media and Blogs Are the Most Rapidly Expanding Category in the Overall Marketing Budget. Social media and blogs are becoming marketing powerhouses. They are the fastest growing category in lead generation budgets and they continue to be ranked as the lowest cost lead-generation channel. In addition, more than any other channel, social media was ranked as a source of leads that has become more important in the last six months.

Businesses Are Generating Real Customers With Social Media and Blogs. Some organizations are still unsure about the utility of social media and blogs. Are potential customers really reading Twitter? Does Facebook do anything more than build brand awareness? The answer is, "Yes"! For Twitter, Facebook, LinkedIn and company blogs, over 40% of our respondents who use those services for marketing have acquired a customer through each of those channels. Social media is not just for brand awareness; it can be used to directly generate leads that translate into customers.

Please understand that because I am writing about an overall strategy, I am only touching the tip of the social media iceberg. As you begin to explore the online terrain, you will discover many new and different ways to extend the reach of your content. There is a great deal of free content on the web related to social media marketing specifically for lawyers, and if the marketers are doing their job, it will be easy for you to find

4. BLOGGING

In his post "Is Blogging the Future of Publishing?," at www.jeffbullas.com, Jeff Bullas says:

Some say it is fading in the face of the social media tsunami and it is passe. I think that in fact the social media universe just amplifies and spreads the influence of blogs through the Digital "World of Mouth".

Blogging is publishing, it is content, and that can be a video, images, text or all of these. Blogging is about niches and allows those that are passionate about their interests to start publishing and sharing online and through promotion drive traffic, eyeballs and then revenue.

Blogging is the democratization of publishing. It allows anyone to publish easily and freely and at low cost and it is becoming a serious business. Blogging is becoming the niche powerhouse of publishing and advertisers will pay good money to market to a tightly targeted and qualified market.

There are many social media authorities who believe blogging is not necessary to create an effective online presence from an SMO standpoint. In general, I would agree that it is not absolutely necessary in social media marketing, but blogging creates an important distinction between social media and content marketing.

If your strategy is based on pushing out informational content, it should include a variety of blog posts, articles, e-books, white papers, videos, podcasts, and other media. Without blog content you have no foundation for your strategy. So when you run into the blog/no-blog debates in the information you'll see during your online participation, you can skip those articles: they don't apply to you!

Grant Griffiths, owner of blogforprofit.com and a partner in the venture StartBloggingToday.com at one time stated:

Blogs build trust and reputation "organically" by allowing potential clients to see the people behind the law practice in action, not mediated by slick marketing. Ironically, this is the most powerful form of marketing there is.

By providing information to the public, you become a trusted and reputable resource. Trusted and reputable resources get clients, period. They also get calls from news media, who are now using the Internet to find sources for their reporting (this often comes as a surprise to many lawyers, but we've seen it happen repeatedly and it is because of blogging). It is well-known in marketing and consumer psychology circles that people prefer to do business with other people they like and who are like them. People cannot like you if they don't know you, and a normal Web site doesn't give them a chance to know you and like you.

These goals are in direct alignment with the goals we discussed in the content/social media segment of this strategy. Trust results from relationship. Relationship results from familiarity and communication. Communication results from participation and transparency. For these reasons, blogging and social media marketing combined produce content marketing that can be extremely powerful, making you stand out from the crowd. This is exciting not only because it is a reliable way to build your practice, but also because you become a presence in the national and international legal community, and this can lead to opportunities you never envisioned.

You can also look at it from an SEO perspective. For analytics purposes, static websites are useless. Google likes moving, changing content. Static websites function now as highly-developed business cards, showcasing, for example, you and your firm's services, areas of expertise, contact information, and the like. But they do not reach out and grab potential clients, and will be found so far back in a search that no one will ever get there. In the study quoted above, it was found that online marketing that included a blog generated 67 percent more business leads than marketing without a blog.

As with the distinctions between social media and content marketing, so there are distinctions between content blogging and building a blogging business. Many bloggers build a business around their blog, selling products and information, using affiliate marketing and other income-generating activities.

Lawyers do not build their practices around blogs. They use the content of their blogs to help build their practices. Different goals, different strategies. Be careful to make the distinction when you research blogging methodology.

But the bottom line is, will blogging help you grow your practice? The answer is yes, and, according to the "Blog Tech Guy" Joel Williams, here's why:

> *Most simply, **a blog helps generate awareness** of what you do, and the services you provide. This means that you have a broader platform to sell from, and more opportunities of getting your message out to your target audience—paying customers.*

> *Blogs are <u>cheap to set up</u>, <u>simple to run</u>, and massively effective. When you think that a simple advert which runs for a week can cost upwards of $250 dollars, a **blog suddenly makes massive financial sense**.*

> *Blogs are one of the few **two-way communications tools** out there which invite your*

customers in to <u>open dialogue</u>. Unlike adverts, brochures and static websites, blogs actively encourage your customers to get in touch and give you feedback. This shows you whether you are on the right track and offers you free advice on how to improve, every day.

Blogs work for you while you are sleeping. *Face to face communication is a great way of generating relationships, but you can't be out and about all the time. Your blog represents you just like a sales rep would working on your behalf, globally, night and day. You have the capacity to open up your services to an instant global market, and let your site do all the hard work for you.*

Blogging is measurable. *Often, when you pay out for advertising or marketing, there is no way of calculating your return on investment. Blogs let you see just how many people are accessing your site, where they come from and when they are looking (use the free **<u>Google Analytics</u>**). It's as if you have a world-class marketing agency at your fingertips at all times, telling you your customer demographic and alerting you to what is effective, and what isn't.*

I recently came across a post by sixteen-year-old Nigerian entrepreneur named Onibalusi Bamidele on www.ariwriter.com called "Blogging with Influence in 5 Easy Steps." They are:

<u>Content</u>: *"Your content is you; you are your content. The power your content can hold, the* *influence it can add to you should not be under-estimated."*

Passion: *"Your passion is a building block for your content. If you seriously have passion for what you do, it will definitely reflect in what you write … Your passion has a lot to do with your content (which is a building block to your influence)."*

Care: *"Do you care for your readers? Caring for your readers is a great element that should not be neglected if truly you want to have great influence on them."*

Authority: *"Let people know you are an authority. You don't need to be subjective but let there be sounds of authority, assurance, and affirmation in anything you write."*

Distinction: *"The final step to influential blogging is distinction. You should be able to distinguish yourself from other bloggers. You should be different."*

This is from a sixteen-year-old kid. Do you think he will succeed at what he does?

Blogging takes courage. Being passionate, transparent, caring, different, and authoritative in your content, and then waving a big red flag around saying "Read me, read me" takes courage. You need to be okay with the fact that some will think you're an idiot, some will disagree with you, and sometimes those people don't keep their opinions to themselves. That's okay; there's lots of room for disagreement among those who participate in this medium and most know it comes with the territory. Don't let it intimidate you. Let it drive you.

We've previously discussed defining both your target audience and your purpose. Your blog must be directed at your ideal clients with the purpose of attracting them to your website, where they will learn more about you and hopefully move through levels of interaction to become your clients.

So we need to answer two questions:
- How are you going to get in front of your potential clients?
- How are you going to lead them to the conclusion that you are the person who can help them?

Accomplishing this requires a combination of developing solid, relevant content and presenting it through a series of relationship-based marketing strategies. In his e-book *New Rules of Viral Marketing*, David Meerman Scott, marketing author, speaker, and social media thought leader, puts it like this:

*For decades, the only way to spread our ideas was to buy expensive advertising or beg the media to write (or broadcast) about our products and services. But now our organizations have a tremendous opportunity to publish great content online—**content that people want to consume and that they are eager to share** with their friends, family, and colleagues. (emphasis added)*

Building your content is the number one thing you must focus on, and it is an ongoing process. Remember that people are interested in themselves and getting their problem solved. You must keep this paramount in your mind: what is the problem your target clients have that you will solve for them? As we said before, your target clients are people who need your help. If you were standing in front of them and asked "How can I help you?" what would they say? Your blog content should reflect how you would respond to their problems.

Content is not only about what you say, but also how you say it. Your job is to attract an audience. That means they must like you, or your blog post is off their screen with the click of a mouse. David Nour, author of *Relationship Economics and Connectability*, advises that you must **influence rather than persuade**. He says: "You must reduce your self-interest, put your own need aside and focus on someone else's concerns." You must listen to what they're saying and respond in a way that shows you did.

Remember Onibalusi, the sixteen-year-old Nigerian? He said "caring for your readers is a great element that should not be neglected if truly you want to have great influence on them."

Think about it this way: if you don't care about the audience of your blog post, how are you ever going to care about your clients? And if you don't care about your clients, why are you doing this for a living, and how do you expect to be successful?

Once you attract your audience, you need to nurture them. You must help people feel good about engaging with you. If they don't feel good about you, they certainly will not be hiring you when they need help. This is your dress rehearsal for the real deal, and the producer's in the audience. Make him or her happy, or the show won't go on.

You may be saying to yourself, this sounds like I need to be phony. Nothing could further from the truth. You need to be totally authentic. You need to find out what your audience is asking, and provide answers or solutions in a way they can understand as well as feel taken care of. That's your job as a blogger and a lawyer.

Here are some ideas that will help you create a blogging presence that combines substance with style:

- <u>Have a conversation with your best friend.</u> You are not interacting with your monitor, or even the (hopefully) masses of people that will read your post. You're talking to your best non-lawyer friend, chatting about an interesting situation he or she encountered and wondered how that would be viewed from a legal perspective. It's a conversation at the end of a golf game over a good, cold beer on a beautiful sunny afternoon. Enjoy yourself.

- <u>Assume your friend knows you and trusts you.</u> You've been friends for fifteen years. There's a reason for that. You're likable, reasonable, and you know your stuff. You know you are held in some esteem by your friend, so there is no reason to shy away from asserting your knowledge with confidence.

- <u>Use a "how to" approach</u>. The majority of on-line searches start with the phrase "How to … "Now, your friend has presented you with a dilemma or a desire. Formulate your response from a practical point of view. What can or should one do in that situation to resolve the dilemma, or what steps should he or she take to achieve the desired result? You can use some limited legal analysis to give credibility to your advice, but only for that reason. Your friend won't benefit from a full-blown diatribe on how the courts have viewed the subject, and doesn't really care.

- <u>Embellish the topic with an example</u>. Giving examples of similar situations and their outcomes shows that you really relate to the topic and feel strongly about it, so much so that you remember once, about ten years ago, when …. Just remember, your example MUST BE FICTIONAL. An amalgamation, perhaps, of several different scenarios. But you must respect your ethical obligations to your clients and your attorney/client privilege, and write with care accordingly.

- <u>Speak from a "preventative" point of view.</u> No one wants to get entangled in a lawsuit any-more—it's just no fun, it costs too much money, and you hardly ever get what you want, anyway. Give your friend advice about how to be sure to avoid the dilemma in the future, or the most important things he or she must do to prevent the lawsuit monster from visiting when he or she engages in whatever conduct you are advising him or her on.

Embrace blogging as an opportunity to help someone, to use your specialized knowledge to advise someone how to stay out of trouble. Play with it, have fun with it. No one will laugh (unless you tell jokes) and if they do, you won't know.

Blogging consistency is an important factor in your blog's success. In the beginning, you need to try to blog three to four times a week. Once you start finding an audience, you can reduce that number, but if you want to keep a steady flow of readers, be sure to write at least once a week.

At times, it is challenging to find new and exciting content to feed your readers, especially if you are short on time. The best way to keep a well full of ideas is to envision yourself as a writer who is always on the lookout for ideas. As you go about your daily life, things happen that may generate a thought about potential content. Keep a folder (digital, physical, or both) and be sure to jot down what went through your mind.

As you participate in social media, you should be reading tweets, blog posts, and other materials avidly. They come from links in tweets, Facebook content and posts in groups on LinkedIn and other sites you may join. Develop the habit of **commenting** on other people's posts as often as you can, and using your comments as a topic for a post of your own. Commenting will not only serve to help develop your own content ideas, but will also raise your online profile. If appropriate, you can link back to one of your own posts for extra exposure; Subscribe to free email updates or RSS feeds from sites such as Law.com, ABA's most relevant sections or divisions, and other law bloggers in your area of expertise to keep up to date on current issues. Set up Google Alerts using keywords for the kind of topics your potential clients will use to search for information. You will receive emails each day containing searches on those keywords. Also use keyword tracking applications such as Google Analytics or www.wordtracker.com to determine what questions your audience is asking.

Some law-related sites, such as www.Avvo.com, allow consumers to ask questions that are answered by lawyers listed on their sites. Make sure your profiles are current at those sites, and answer questions as another way to raise your online profile. But also use those questions to create relevant content for your blog.

JDSupra.com, an online legal publisher that we will talk about further in the syndication discussion, offers a great service for a small monthly fee. This service not only automatically syndicates your blog post in several areas, but also provides a list of trending topics in your area of expertise.

Another integral aspect of successful blogging is **linking** to other blogs or to previous posts within your own site. Linking is the fundamental basis of the web. Links help you be recognized as an expert in your field, direct traffic to your site, and increase your visibility on the web. Search engines want to know you're sufficiently "connected" with other pages and content, so linking out to other pages matters for SEO. Engaging in dialogue with the owners or staff of relevant content sites in your niche is a great way to get noticed, and it can lead to links back to you. Bloggers definitely watch who is linking to them, and you can take the initiative by linking out *first* before looking for one in return.

Simply linking out for the sake of linking won't accomplish much, especially with bloggers who gets lots of links. The key is to be strategic about how you link and what you say. Here are some rules of thumb for linking based on generally accepted best practices:

- Link to relevant content fairly early in the body copy
- Link to relevant pages approximately every 120 words of content
- Link to relevant *interior* pages of your site or other sites
- Link with naturally relevant anchor text

Don't get stuck on rules, but be aware of what works, and use it as much as you can while focusing primarily on good content and engagement. I use the SEO tool from ScribeSEO.com._Once you've written your post, set up your keywords, tags, and categories, click on the analyze button and Scribe will score your post for SEO and tell you what to do to score higher. For a minimal monthly fee, you don't need to give SEO a thought until the end, and you know exactly what to do to get the best SEO possible.

5. GUEST BLOGGING

Guest blogging is a great way to get yourself front and center. Once you've established relationships with other law bloggers, offer to write a guest post for them. I promise they will love you, and you will have created an additional source of exposure to enhance your prospects of gaining a wider readership.

6. COMMENTING

Comments to your blogs give you the best opportunity to connect directly with your audience. Be sure to make it easy for readers to comment. Never close comments, and always respond to them. Remember, you're trying to create conversation that can lead to getting clients. Although there are quite a few steps in between the two events, it cannot start without the conversation. Grab it where you can.

Commenting on other people's blogs is another way to assert point of view and give yourself more relevance. Reaching out in some way to your online niche shows you have ideas and information, and ideas about the information. These are the qualities of a thought leader.

So then there's always the question: for marketing purposes, does it work? I don't think there's a quantifiable way you can ever measure the ROI of this kind of marketing. There's just no way to determine how many people were affected or motivated by your online efforts. However, Hubspot.com conducted a study called "The State of Inbound Lead Generation," which revealed that of the businesses they studied, those who blogged regularly generated 67 percent more leads for their business. Grant Griffiths blogs about the study on his Blog for Profit site.

There is much more to successful blogging than I've included here. I've given you the aerial view of the blogosphere, but there's much more information to be gained by zooming in on the specifics. Be prepared to read instructive blogs and e-books; these are typically either free or very inexpensive. Join an online group or take an online course to learn more in-depth blogging strategies. My recommendations are the following:

- Grant Griffiths:BlogforProfit.com and Start-BloggingToday.com
- Michael Martine: www.Remarkablogger.com
- Darren Rowse: www.problogger.com
- Brian Clark: www.copyblogger.com
- David Risley: www.DavidRisley.com

Each of them is a master blogger, and Grant, a former lawyer, in particular gives great guidance to lawyers. The others serve up the best blogging perspectives and strategies around, but remember that they may be talking to the "blogging as a business" audience.

Other resources specific to content marketing are www.Junta42.com and its instructional arm, www.ContentMarketingInstitute.com, as well as www.Legal-MediaMatters.com and www.Conduit.com.

CHAPTER 6

CONTENT MARKETING, PART 2

1. SYNDICATING YOUR BLOG POST

Earlier we discussed getting involved in social media before you do anything to launch your practice. The purpose of that was to get you warmed up and familiar with the various sites, how they work, how others use them, and how they can now help you get exposure for your posts by contributing them to your social communities. Now it's time to create your "buzz" on the web.

Publishing a blog post on your website can create some traffic if you use good SEO strategies. But keep in mind that there are hundreds of thousands of blogs; good SEO can only get you so far. As we discussed, content marketing requires both SEO and SMO.

Well-optimized websites will include social media buttons that allow your reader to share content and connect with the site owner/blog author on social media. Be sure only to include the share functions for sites you actually participate on—but be sure to include them.

A post without a retweet button next to it is like a prom queen without a date: all dressed up, and nowhere to go. Likewise, your site should include buttons to share content on Facebook, as well as a Facebook follow to connect readers to your profile or page.

Good SMO also requires that you get your post out on other sites that publish content, or that direct readers to your post by linking back to your site. There are a significant number of law-related social network sites that you can join and contribute to. For purposes of this discussion, I am going to focus on the three top social media giants: Twitter, Facebook and LinkedIn, as well as four law-related content publishers: MartindaleConnected, JDSupra, myLegal and Avvo. Please remember, however, that social media changes with the speed of technology, which functions in the immediate present. When those changes happen, you need to change with them.

In order to make the syndication process run smoothly, one thing you need to know about are URL shorteners. URL shorteners do just that: shorten the URL of the post or website you want to link to. If the vehicle you are using does not shorten URLs automatically, you need to subscribe to one (it's very simple and costs nothing). Google "URL shorteners" and your search will bring up a variety of them. Bit.ly appears to be the most popular, is very reliable, and has the added function of showing your history of how many hits you've had on the URLs you've shortened. But investigate others such as TinyURL or ht.ly to see what works best for you.

- **Twitter** Once you have published your post, be sure to publish a link to it via Twitter. If Wordpress is your blogging platform, you can install a plug-in and automate this function upon publication, or you can do it manually. I use a Twitter management tool called Hootsuite that has a "hootlet," or syndication button you can install on your toolbar. If you click the hootlet button on your post page, it will populate a tweet with a short title in combination with a URL shortener. You can also set up Hootsuite to send the post link out to your Facebook profile and page and LinkedIn at the same time, and edit the tweet if you want to add or delete what is automatically included. Hootsuite also enables you to send now, or schedule a tweet for later. Since information on Twitter is pretty much a moving target, it is helpful to schedule several tweets for your new post over time to catch different audiences and allow for time-zone differences. Be sure to entitle it "new blog post" to increase potential re-tweet action. (Note: There are several additional social media management tools that enable you to syndicate your message across various platforms: Tweetdeck, Seesmic, co-Tweet and Ping are among the most popular.)

- **Facebook** If you have chosen to set up a business page in addition to your profile, be sure post a link to the post on both pages. Do this manually so your status update will be more prominent. Alternatively, you can use an application called NetworkedBlogs, which automatically feeds your new post to both pages when you register with them.
- **LinkedIn** LinkedIn provides for automatic feeds from Wordpress and other blogging

platforms, so be sure to set up this feature, and your posts will appear on your profile page. Additionally, add your new post links to the discussion section of the relevant groups you belong to. Be sure to click the box that says "follow this discussion" so you are notified of and can respond to any comments you receive. LinkedIn groups really expand your audience, so be sure not to skip this step.

- **JDSupra** Publish your post, court, or transactional documents on their main site, as well as their Facebook pages and LinkedIn groups. If you sign up for their monthly service, they will do all that for you. JDSupra has a huge searchable library and readership, and recently collaborated with LinkedIn to create Legal Updates. This service enables you to upload and distribute your documents directly on LinkedIn once you install the link (instructions are on their main site).

- **Martindale Connected** MC membership includes anyone employed in the law and legal services industries, and is a significant source of referral business as well as an additional source of exposure. Again, upload your post to both your profile blog as well as in the forum section of the groups you belong to, and be sure to receive notifications of any comments you may receive.

- **myLegal** is a focused community and marketing site for lawyers and legal vendors with innovative tools to leverage your onsite presence to increase your business. The site has recently added several unique functions, such as their elearning portal, to create diverse ways to showcase their knowledge, skills and products. You can upload your blog posts, podcasts and advertise your events, connect directly with LinkedIn and integrate with Digital War Room right within the site. It is emerging as an aggressive and unique platform to accomplish tasks typically spread across a variety of sites.

- **Avvo** is a great site to join and become active on. This site enables consumers to ask questions, research site content, and search for lawyers. Avvo gives lawyers the opportunity to answer questions in their areas of expertise and contribute to its "Legal Guides," or what I call "how-to" blog posts. They also have a rating system based on your contributions, which is the subject of some controversy. But since Avvo includes a listing on all lawyers, whether or not they have joined the site, it is best to control the information about yourself by at least completing your profile. Answering questions, however, is a great way to reach potential clients directly. And an easy way to contribute is to reproduce your blog post in a how-to format.

There are many other social and law-related networking sites that offer publishing opportunities. More often than not, these are community-related sites where the purpose is to provide for interaction among the membership. However, remember this is a social game. Any opportunity you have to interact with colleagues, vendors, and other members of the legal services industry is a chance for a new contact or referral.

This process can be fairly time-consuming. If you are just starting out, however, this is your job right now. You need to work just as hard at this marketing process as you will when your practice flourishes. As your practice becomes financially viable, you will be able to hire an assistant, virtual or otherwise, to help with the technical aspects of this process.

2. USING SUBSCRIPTION TOOLS AND EMAIL MARKETING TO CREATE YOUR COMMUNITY

The main purpose of inbound marketing, educational or otherwise, is to *capture the contact information* of the people who are reading your material. On social networking sites, people follow, "friend," or connect with you in whatever fashion that site enables them to. But how do you connect with your anonymous readers? How do you stay on their radar? The key is to get their email addresses.

Email services such as www.aWeber.com and www. ConstantContact.com provide the systems and structures for you to set up an email subscription service on your website, at a minimal monthly cost. They will notify you when you have a subscriber. Once the list starts, you can set up email campaigns through their autoresponders, which will automatically send out a series of emails with content you create and at intervals you designate. These can be newsletters, alerts, or just a straight-up email that contains extra information, such as links to news, blogs, or other data you may have retweeted or posted on Facebook. Content can be short and informal, and can include what's going on at your office, what you're doing for a holiday, or whatever might give your readers a better glimpse of who you are. You can find lots of information on awesome email campaigns through your email service or online marketers (for free, of course).

Last, your blog should also include the opportunity for readers to subscribe through an RSS feed such as www.feedburner.com or www.feedblitz.com. Although you cannot obtain contact information when people subscribe through an RSS, you can check your stats through your service to see, for example, how many people subscribed to a particular post. This provides direction on which posts are more popular than others. There are many other analytics you can gain by visiting your feedburner dashboard, if you like that kind of input.

3. REPURPOSING AND BEING CREATIVE WITH YOUR BLOG CONTENT

As a vehicle for creating content, blogging is not the only game in town. Notice that many blog sites you visit also include articles, white papers and e-books for downloading, or use video and podcast formats. You will need to move into these content-creation mediums when you are ready.

More writing, you say? More new ideas? Not necessarily. Your blog content can be repurposed for these mediums. For great tips on some easy repurposing, read "3 Simple Ways to Repurpose Your Blog Posts for More Exposure" by Denise Wakeman. Here are several idea examples:

- You've written several posts on the same topic, but covering a different aspect of that topic. Gather these posts together and create an e-book. You can then offer the ebook for free as an enticement to subscribe to your blog, or as an added value to your subscribers through a special email offering.
- You've written a post about something that has since changed in some way. Continue the post and turn it into an article. You can offer the article in the same way as the e-book, or try to publish it in an online article aggregator such as www.ezine.com, or other law-related online magazines.
- You've just completed analysis of a business structure that reflected a legal trend that would be helpful to your target market.

Using video, podcasts, webinars, and other forms of audio/video content are very popular forms of communication for many reasons. Videos are very inexpensive to make, stay online forever, and are far more search-engine friendly that the written word. Webinars, podcasts, and other broadcasting vehicles allow you to create dynamic content that is more engaging and interactive.

Learning how to make good videos is important, but it's fairly easy using your computer's video capabilities or a simple flip camera. Remember, this is not prime time, and a high degree of professionalism is not expected. In fact, there is a certain degree of charm in spontaneity and vulnerability, so don't be afraid to just be yourself. Once you've got your technique down and are ready to take another step to expand your audience,, you can embed them into your blog platform and upload them onto your YouTube channel or other video syndicator such as www.vimeo.com, www.viddler.com, www.uStream.com, and others. uStream also has a free download producer application that enhances your existing video capabilities.

You can create your own radio show by using your computer, a microphone, and podcasting software. Everything you need to know about how to create and publish your podcast can be found at www.howstuffworks.com. Podcasts can also be created through third-party services such as www.blogtalkradio.com or www.legaltalknetwork.com by purchasing your own channel, if you intend to podcast on a continuous basis.

4. CONDUCTING WEBINARS

Webinars are used as an instructional or interview event in which content goes beyond the scope of a blog post. They are broadcast at specific dates and times, although recordings of the webinar are generally provided to registrants after the live event, and can be embedded on your website for later viewing by newcomers. Their format provides for audio instruction combined with Slideshare or other presentations, and can include live interaction with your audience or answering questions written and submitted through a chat function. They are created through various services, which vary in price and function related to publicity, analytics, and other related activities. The most popular services are: www.BrightTalk.com, www.GoToWebinar.com, and www.InstantTeleseminar.net. A newer service, InstantPresenter, includes a video component in its webinar broadcast platform.

Webinars enable you to interact with subscribers on a multi-media level that leads to increased likelihood of continued contact. I find having a conversation with a guest on a webinar to be more relaxing than giving a presentation. You may want to encourage the audience to participate and ask questions so that the conversation extends out to include them. That is the beginning of relationship that could lead to gaining a client when the person needs you.

These audio/video publication methods provide a wide range of opportunities to expand your audience and your contact list, and reach further into your target market areas. They enable you to attract that growing segment of your market that is not enticed by reading, even when it's online. But don't pressure yourself to learn all of this right away. As you will see, you have a lot more to think about when getting your new practice up and running.

CHAPTER 7:

ALTERNATIVE FEE AGREEMENTS: THE FACE OF OPPORTUNITY

In a blog post entitled "How to Compete on Price," Jordan Furlong concludes:

> *It probably goes without saying that the single biggest inefficiency in most law firms is the fact that tasks are worth more the longer they take and the more resources they consume. Hourly billing—and more importantly in this context, hourly compensation—is a productivity hemorrhage that's becoming far more damaging to firms than to clients. And it is not sustainable.*

We all know this in our hearts, yet law firms hang on to the billable hour model for dear life. In his article "The Billable Hour: How Sick Is It?" Jim Hassett says:

> *In every profession, sellers love the billable hour, because it puts all the risk on the buyer side. Believe me, if I could sell all of my company's services on an hourly basis, I would switch over in a heartbeat. But I'm stuck with fixed price work, because I sell to lawyers, and they hate buying services by the hour. They know better.*

121

1. THE UNSUSTAINABILITY OF THE BILLABLE HOUR

The billable hour made its entry on the legal stage somewhere between the 1940s and the 1960s. Before that, according to Will Auther, partner at Bowman and Brook, a client would retain an attorney to perform specific services which were outlined in an agreement. When the services were complete, the attorney would bill the client a lump sum based on the value of the work, and the client would pay it.

Then the law firm met the insurance company, which saw legal services as a commodity that could be valued according to the time it took to perform them, and the billable hour was born.

But over the past sixty years, law firms continued to raise their hourly rates to levels where, in a recessionary market, law clients cannot afford and have often been forced to appear in court pro se. So now, among the vagaries of a recession-fueled legal market comes the demand for a change in lawyers' traditional billing structure.

Legal fees are being scrutinized and challenged not only by individuals and small business, but also by in-house counsel, who are being forced to cut costs. Individual and small business clients are refusing to agree to open-ended hourly billing at astronomical rates. Moreover, corporate clients are demanding a restructure of billing methods from outside counsel. In his blog post "Alternative Fee Arrangements: Part 1," Jerome Kowalski writes:

> *The data base recently announced by a signifi-*
> *cant group of corporate counsel (the "ACC Val-*
> *ue Index") under which law firms will be rated*
> *by clients on a scale of one to five for six criteria:*
> *([1] understanding objectives/expectations;*
> *[2] legal expertise; [3] efficiency/process man-*
> *agement; [4] responsiveness/communications;*
> *[5] predictable cost budgeting skills; and [6]*
> *results delivered/execution and this data base*
> *will be available for all corporate counsel.*

Yet, when FMC Technologies, Inc., an oil and gas company, posted a request on www.LegalOnRamp.com,
for proposals from tech-savvy, innovative firms that
were open to alternative billing arrangements, they
received only fifty responses. An FMC representative
stated in "Few Large Firms Answer FMC's Calls for Help,"
June 15, 2009, on amlawdaily.typepad.com that:

> *… a cynic might conclude that the vast majority*
> *of firms chose not to respond because they are*
> *neither willing nor able to embrace a changing*
> *competitive landscape where customers want*
> *new legal service delivery models.*

The problem? Jay Shepard of The Shepard Group, an
employment law firm in Boston that bills only by fixed
fees, puts it like this:

> *Think of alternative billing not just as a change*
> *in your billing. Think of it as a fundamental*
> *change in your business model.*

In other words, lawyers are not prepared to reorganize
the financial underpinnings of their practice unless absolutely forced to do so.

Jordan Furlong, in "METAMORPHOSIS: Five Forces Transforming the Legal Services Marketplace," says:

> ... more and more firms are discussing the institution of fixed-fee billing regimes. This will be a challenge for many because, in law firms, internal cost is the driver of external price, whereas in most marketplaces, it's the other way around. Nonetheless, in future, "price" will be what the market will pay and "cost" will be whatever the firm incurs to deliver its services; profit (or loss) will be the difference between the two. As a result, firms will increasingly have to streamline their costs of production, resulting in much greater systematization of legal services delivery.

For a large, established law firm, this is not an easy task. The entire law firm culture and financial structure is built around the number of hours billed by each associate per year. In their article "Alternative Fee Arrangements: Risk Sharing Requires a Strong Partnership," James A. Comodeca and Scott R. Everett of Dinsmore & Shohl, LLP, say:

> ... the change required for many firms to succeed should not be taken lightly. Law firms must adapt a new skill set which can generally be described as project management: developing reliable forecasting methods, pushing cost accountability to the lowest process of legal work, and establishing relationships with clients that lead to open and honest communication. To a business executive, these areas have long been required for running a market-leading organization.

Even in the face of this uproar, big law has made it clear that they intend to increase their hourly fees, leading to what Jordan Furlong calls "The Boutique Exodus":

> *What's happening now, however, is that the clients and their lawyers are teaming up and doing an end run around the firms …. It's a four-step process: client tells lawyer it can't afford her rates anymore. Lawyer tells client she doesn't control her rates and doesn't want to lose the client. Light bulbs appear simultaneously over their heads. And a few months later, a new small firm is born, with at least one A-list client on its roster … It's also no coincidence that in many of these new firms, lawyers are selling their services on a flexible- or flat-fee basis. That's the new reality of the lawyer-client relationship, and these boutiques are among the first to get it.*

Consumers and corporate counsel alike are demanding more value from the legal services they receive. The Association for Corporate Counsel, in a white paper entitled "The ACC Value Based Fee Primer," says:

> *Over the past ten years, overall costs to U.S. companies rose 20%, while legal costs rose 75%. In fact, legal fees have continued to escalate through the recent recession. While the global economic crisis forced many producers to hold prices flat or even reduce them, on average U.S. law firms actually increased hourly billing rates during the "Great Recession" of 2009. Moreover, in a recent survey, approximately 90% of law firm respondents said they will raise rates in 2010.*

What impact is this having? Corporate counsel describe their "single largest unmet need" as "better value from law firms." And the concerns are not limited to the General Counsels' office. Fifty-four percent of CEOs / CFOs in another survey stated they are "very highly" or "highly" interested in reducing outside counsel costs.

Against this backdrop, value-based fee structures are seen as an effective way to manage cost. But it goes beyond just the dollars. Many have described it as an improved approach to management necessary in a more competitive global business environment. This is especially true in companies where other divisions have increased productivity via innovative use of technology, knowledge sharing and similar management tools—all to improve the company's bottom line. The refrain that "legal is different" is increasingly falling upon deaf ears.

This, in a nutshell, represents the "business case" for value-based fee structures. *It creates incentives to:*

- *reduce inefficiencies*
- *increase productivity*
- *improve the way legal services are purchased and delivered, and*
- *focus on results and outcomes that add value for the corporate client.*

If you have not yet been asked to focus on these goals, chances are the request—or the mandate—will come soon. That is precisely when this resource can help.

2. THE PROBLEM WITH THE BILLABLE HOUR

The shift from the billable hour to alternative pricing is not about money. It's about two things:

- how you perceive your work, and
- how you perceive your relationship with your client

If anything, the billable hour has served to commoditize work product by assigning value to it in terms of the time it took to produce it. The value of the work lawyers perform is related to the special skills and knowledge we bring to bear upon a client's circumstances to enable resolution. How long that process takes has no bearing upon the worth of those skills and knowledge.

The billable hour system has had a divisive effect on the attorney/client relationship. The legal process can be extremely laborious and time-intensive if you enter into it with an adversarial posture rather than focusing on resolution or desired result. As attorneys, we can get consumed by the procedural power of our craft. The more we practice with an attitude of flexing our muscles, the more costly our services become when based on the billable hour system. The client, not knowing what is or is not really necessary to complete the assignment, lives in fear of uncertain costs his or her lack of power to control them.

The problems created by a billable hour system can be summarized as follows:

- It demeans our work by categorizing what we do as a service. We are knowledge providers.

We sell intellectual capital and innovation to get the best possible results for our clients. Our knowledge has intrinsic value. It has nothing to do with how long it takes to apply our knowledge to our client's circumstances and create solutions. The pricing of our product must relate to the value the client places on that solution.

- It creates a conflict of interest between attorney and client. When law firm profitability and partnership shares are tied to numbers of hours billed, it is the attorney's best interest to take longer to perform tasks, whereas the opposite is in the client's best interest.

- It rewards inefficient workflow, reinvented wheels, maximized activity, and over-accomplished tasks.

- It creates a level of suspicion and distrust on the part of the client. Instead of creating a working partnership with our client, there is an underlying atmosphere of conflict in which clients are constantly requiring justification for our work that we must defend.

- The client is forced to live with the uncertainty of an open-ended financial obligation, and must bear all the risk associated with the cost of legal services we provide.

- Not all time spent requires the same level of skill. Researching, formulating legal theories of the case, and drafting complex documents have far more value than preparing a motion for filing, yet all of these tasks are billed at the same hourly rate.

In his blog post "Alternative Fees, Part 1: What's Wrong with Billing by the Hour," Jim Hassett discusses further issues raised by the billable hour model, and recent findings of the drawbacks caused by its use.

3. THE FACE OF OPPORTUNITY

What do I see when I look at these realities? The face of opportunity. If a big-firm associate exodus can make an end-run around their former employers, so can sole practitioners and small firms. Newly-formed law practices have a huge advantage over big law: they are not institutionalized. They have no framework, no structures, no traditions to dismantle. They do not carry the burden of keeping a behemoth business functioning as they break down the old and institute the new.

In a previous discussion, we talked briefly about the fact that operating virtually "levels the playing field." It costs next to nothing to get a VLO up and running. Many web 2.0 productivity products are free or nearly free. Content marketing costs next to nothing to create online visibility, where your clients are searching for you. **In short, these methods provide an extremely cost-effective strategy to run your practice, allowing you the luxury of offering the number one demand of clients for legal services: certainty in their legal costs.**

4. EFFICIENCY AND COST CONTAINMENT

Alternative pricing of legal services also isn't just about pricing; it requires streamlining your practice to create efficiency and contain costs. Besides the monstrosity of a job it takes to reinvent a large law firm based on pricing other than billable hours, these firms are also resistant because they are afraid: afraid of the unknown and afraid to take risks. Since law firms have never been efficient or cost-effective, their fears may be well-founded. Law firms have gotten away with raising their hourly rates year after year, and their costs are hardly ever considered. In short, if law firms had to compete in the business world, they would fail miserably.

Now, law practices must align their business model with traditional business concepts. They are losing clients who have suffered as a result of the recession and can no longer afford to take on uncertain and overpriced legal fees. Law firms cannot afford to reduce their rates or create fee structures that shift the cost risk from the client to the firm, because they have not addressed cost containment. The reality is, clients don't care about your costs, and costs should not be a factor in pricing your work.

Law firms have begun to admit that they never really engaged in developing a cost analysis of the legal product. They have simply followed a strategy of hiring lots of associates and setting billable hour requirements that will finance the firm's operations. When you are in a marketplace stressed by unemployment and reduced spending patterns, that system doesn't work.

So let's just say your position is: I understand this is important, but I don't know what exactly to do to respond. How should I change? Where do I start? Here are some fundamental building blocks on which to structure your firm's practice:

- Remember you are a **business owner.** Your practice needs to be tended like a business, not a semi-collegiate institution where finding some arcane legal theory is cause for an open-bar celebration at 5 pm. Legal theory is interesting, and by all means use what you need, but no more. Your clients won't pay for it.
- Think **cost containment**. Pure and simple. Before you make a decision about anything to do with how you practice, the first question you must ask yourself is: is incorporating this method the least costly way I can accomplish my goal? And I'm not talking about buying the cheapest laptop or the lowest service level of an application. Containing costs takes planning. It takes reviewing the last year's worth of monthly expenses to track where the money is going, and what can be cut out to bring it within your income and profit goals for that period of time.
- Closely tied to cost containment is **efficiency.** Where is your time being wasted? How can you eliminate that? Conduct a similar review of your staff's time. Analyze how work flows through your office: is there a system by which a client's matter moves through the legal processes it requires in an orderly fashion? Are there ways in which each person who handles the file (lawyer or staff) can quickly access the information about the matter so they can do their part? If not, efficiently create these systems by using:
- **Technology**. There are dozens of cloud applications designed specifically for lawyers 131

that streamline your workflow once the necessary information is input. I'm talking about practice management, case management, time/billing, scheduling, collaboration and any other number tools that house all of your information, documents, communications securely so you don't have to. What about desktop programs? They're out there, of course, but all the IT developer talent is going to the cloud. Businesses are adopting cloud applications over desktop in huge numbers. And you know why? Because they're **cost effective.** Technology can also provide you with **legal project management** software that will give you a structure in which you can create an efficiency model to keep you on track. **Mind-mapping** technology helps you create your legal strategy, and keeps you from needing to rethink it over and over. It also provides the comfort that, if something is found that requires a change of strategy, you can go back and throw it into the original thought process to see how that affects your course of action.

These are some of the basic concepts you must consider when preparing your firm to succeed in the very near future. It takes some getting used to. But once you integrate these concepts into your thinking and planning, you will begin to see their usefulness in many different ways, not the least of which to keep your mind empty of business issues when it should be.

5. THE BENEFITS OF ALTERNATIVE PRICING

Although the billable hour pricing model provides a solid income stream which law firms have found reliable, it has also created a state of anxiety and frustration for the client and the lawyer who is serving that client. As long as there is any level of mistrust between attorney and client, the entire relationship is fraught with mutual disquiet and resentment.

I recall an associate position I once had in a small boutique real estate firm, where there were two partners and three associates. The partner I worked under was quite trigger-happy, and I spent my time (and clients' money) engaged in producing motions and discovery that were unnecessary. I was mortified every time I met with clients because I knew they were being "over-represented," and I was exasperated every time my boss told me to write another set of interrogatories. As I recall, that was the last law firm position I ever had. I knew there had to be a better way.

In the article "Alternative Fees for Litigation: Improved Control and Higher Value," James D. Shomper and Gardner G. Courson state:

> *Alternative fee agreements, though not a panacea, do provide a mechanism for law firms and clients to redefine their relationship in fundamental ways that can prove mutually beneficial. Corporate legal departments are under increasing pressure from their clients to reduce costs and justify expenditures. Hourly rates, with their built-in inefficiencies, are a prime*

133

target for reform. Past efforts at cost control- for example, managing costs by micromanaging specific tasks and time entries billed by outside counsel-have achieved at best relatively modest savings at the expense of undermining any true partnering relationship. Far greater savings are likely to be gained by creating billing arrangements that incorporate mutually defined objectives, provide incentives to obtain these common objectives, and encourage efficiency in getting there.

In its most progressive form, an alternative fee arrangement would provide for mutual sharing of risks and rewards. No longer would the client be the sole party to risk cost overruns or a "bad" result. The law firm would share those risks in some manner, while at the same time sharing the potential rewards for attaining clearly defined business objectives. In this paradigm of mutual risk and reward sharing, the interests of client and law firm are aligned toward a common goal.

There is a level of mutual trust that grows between attorney and client when there is willingness to share the risk of both the profit and the outcome. This is the kind of environment in which long-term relationships develop. When an attorney or law firm is willing to consider the undue burden borne by the client in a billable-hour arrangement by offering alternative fee structures, there is the intangible benefit of the evolution of a dedicated relationship.

When attorneys and clients align their goals and understandings, the conflict of interest related to the efficiency with which legal representation is provided is eliminated. Attorneys are on the same side of the cost-containment issue as are the clients. Moreover, our work as lawyers becomes no longer simply a commodity of time. The knowledge, analysis, and legal insight we bring to bear on the client's matter is valued, and our perception of ourselves as lawyers is enhanced.

6. IF NOT THE BILLABLE HOUR, THEN WHAT?

So the question now is, how do you price your work if not by the hour? The tendency is to simply estimate the time you anticipate will be required in performing the legal work, multiply that by your hourly rate, and come up with a final fixed fee. But there are two problems with that approach:

- your estimation of your time is just that: only an estimate. If it takes longer, you'll feel like you lost money and be resentful. If fewer hours are necessary, you're cheating your client.
- it doesn't embody the underlying focus shifts from service provider to knowledge provider, and from lawyer-centric to client-centric. In fact, it is simply the billable hour wrapped up in a nice package with a neat new bow.

Unfortunately, there is no real pricing model for selling intellectual capital. Knowledge is intangible, and manifests itself only in the result it can attain through its use in a specific way. Since it is not unusual for even the best and brightest lawyers, performing the best work and producing the best work product, to achieve a less-than-desirable outcome for their clients, desired results cannot be guaranteed. They can only be strived for.

A variety of alternative fee structures have been used, including:
- Fee caps
- Discounted fees with performance bonus
- Success fees
- Holdbacks
- Blended rates
- Volume discounts
- Full contingency
- Fixed fees
- Subscription fees
- Portfolio billing

Kevin Houchin, founder of The Space Between Center for Creative Spirit in Business and Attorney at Houchin & Associates, P.C., has been extremely successful in using monthly subscription fees as his pricing model. Kevin, a business lawyer, charges a monthly fee for the ongoing legal services he provides to his business clients. The fee is set depending on the scope of work they are retaining him to perform, the size of the business, and a variety of other factors. Other lawyers who have adopted his approach by learning it through Kevin's The Space Between Center, and are excited about how this model has changed the entire nature of their practice and enabled them to enjoy their client relationships.

The monthly subscription fee works well when you are a business lawyer serving clients who have need for ongoing legal advice and work product. There may be other areas of law that would find this model useful as well. However, it is not a generalized pricing system that can be used in all types of legal engagement.

Similar to the subscription model is portfolio billing. In "Portfolio Billing: A Valuable Option for Solos, Small Firms," Correy Stephenson describes portfolio billing as:

> *an arrangement where a law firm takes on all the legal work—or a specific subset of legal work, like all employment litigation, for example—for a client at a flat fee ... Portfolio billing provides "steadier cash flow and a steadier flow of work," and offers lawyers "an opportunity to distinguish themselves" to clients, said Allison Shields, president of Legal Ease Consulting in Port Jefferson, N.Y. ... Instead of doing more work to increase the number of billable hours on a case, portfolio billing encourages lawyers to resolve matters more efficiently, said Shields, something clients can appreciate.*

7. VALUE PRICING: CHANGING YOUR BUSINESS MODEL

But the model that most comprehensively incorporates solutions to the problems raised by the billable hour structure and achieves the results sought by pricing alternatives is fixed fees based on value pricing. It is not the easiest path to take but it is the most successful in aligning the interests of lawyer and client, fostering an atmosphere of trust, creating efficiency, and engaging otherwise reticent clients. Recently, Jay Shepherd wrote a blog post entitled "Two Kinds of Lawyers," in which he said:

There are only two kinds of lawyers in the world:

Lawyers who price, and lawyers who don't. Everything else is lip service, or window dressing, or sleight of hand.

Ron Baker is one of the founders of the Verasage Institute, a think tank dedicated to promulgating and teaching value pricing, customer economics, and human capital development to professionals and businesses around the world. He has developed an eight-point approach to pricing a client's legal matter based on the valuation of professional knowledge and partnership with the client. His theories underscore many of the tenets of value pricing.

From an internal perspective, value pricing is based on how you perceive the value of your contribution. What do you think you're worth? What is the value of your ability to be innovative and to creatively achieve desired results? Remember that every lawyer is different, and what you do is wrapped up in who you are. You can charge a premium for those things that are special about you.

From an external perspective, value pricing is based on the maximum amount a customer will pay in the marketplace, according to and affected by location, financial cycles, and competition. This needs to be put in the mix as well.

Look at your pricing from the clients' perspective. What is it that clients really want? They're not buying a motion for summary judgment or contract for sale of a business. They're buying solutions to their problems and the ability to sleep at night. They are buying expectations, and it is your job to determine what they are and to develop a course of action to reach them.

For those reasons, the first conversation you have with your new client is the most important one. You need to dig deep, not just into the facts and circumstances of the legal matter at hand, but also into their price sensitivities, their emotions, their finances, their level of distress. *Because the higher level of service they will require, the higher the price of the work. The more commoditized the nature of the work is to be performed, the lower the price.* Think about the aspects of the work that would demand premium pricing: the certainty of the cost of your services is always a premium point (think higher interest rates for a thirty-year fixed loan). The urgency of the matter should also be considered, if rush service is required.

Once you've had this conversation and followed the steps outlined below, you present the price of the work to the client up front, as opposed to the billable hour model that increases clients' costs over time. You need to stand firm on your price unless you are willing to allow the client to have control over your billing model. Chances are, if the client requests changes in your initial price determination, he or she may continue to do so down the line. That is not in line with the trust relationship you are looking for.

Jay Shepard's employment law firm, The Shepard Group, operates exclusively on value pricing. Jay outlines eleven factors to consider in setting prices:

- <u>Analyze the client</u>: Is he or she a sophisticated consumer of legal services?

139

- <u>Assess the importance of the matter</u>: Severity, timing, chance of prevailing.
- <u>Urgency</u>: Charge a premium if the matter requires immediate action.
- <u>Competitors</u>: Pay attention to what they would charge, but don't mimic it
- <u>Consider different possible outcomes</u>: Determine what the stakes are.
- <u>Consider difficulty in getting service elsewhere</u>: Is this commoditized work that could be performed by any number of other lawyers, or does it require your expertise, making it difficult to find comparable quality elsewhere?
- <u>Importance of your expertise to outcome</u>: Is this a slam-dunk winner or loser? Or are there issues that depend on a certain level of expertise to prevail on?
- <u>Consider past charges for similar work</u>: Were they too high or too low in retrospect?
- <u>Consider likelihood of referrals from client</u>: If this client will return or refer work to you, it makes sense to price it in a way to encourage him or her to do that; but be careful, you don't want to lock yourself into an unsustainably low price for future work.
- <u>How much work have you done for this client in the past?</u> Always take care of loyal customers.
- <u>How important is it to get this case for the firm?</u> If you are ambivalent, charge more.
- <u>What is the economic benefit to the client to have the problem solved?</u> What would be the client's cost if it was not solved?

Never price the matter on the spot, on the phone, or via email. You need to do some due diligence to learn about the case, the client, and the urgency of the matter. Obtain documents from the client and review them, ask many questions, and spell out the scope and value (or price) in a written agreement. Follow the steps in the pricing processed proposed by Ron Baker:

- During your initial consultation, determine the client's level of expectation and understanding of the scope of work involved. Be specific. Understand what it is about the circumstances that keep him or her awake at night. The higher the level of expectations, the greater the value of your work.
- Review the results of your consultation with a pricing partner. This could be a business partner, a friend, or whomever you rely on to help you make decisions. Never make this decision by yourself. When pricing, be sure to add a premium for pricing certainty.
- Develop three pricing options, each one based on a particular client's expectations: your walk-away price (if the client won't agree to this, you won't take the case; this is the lowest level of expectation price); your hoped-for price (highest level of expectation and access); and your aspiration price (somewhere between the two).
- Present pricing options to the client, using an analogy to compare the three prices (e.g., Where do you want to sit on the plane?).
- Codify the client's choice in a fixed price agreement. Be sure to include all the specifics of the

scope of work, payment terms, timeline, degree of access.

- Do not delay billing the client according to the payment terms, and do not begin work until you've received the full or first installment payment.

- Conduct a before-action review with anyone who will work with you on the matter to discuss intended results, anticipated challenges, what has been learned in similar situations, and what action will make this successful.

- Do not permit "scope creep." If the client requests or agrees to performance outside the scope of the agreement, execute a change order. But think carefully as to whether or not you should have anticipated the additional work or change of scope in your original proposal.

- Conduct an after-action review, or debriefing, to reflect on what you have done, how you added value, what more could be done in the future, etc. This is essential, as it will force you to address these issues in the future.

In "Pricing on Purpose: How to Implement Value Pricing in Your Firm," Ron Baker defines eleven specific steps to take, addressing issues such as "Questions to Ask the Client" and "20 Questions the Pricing Council Should Ask Itself Before Establishing a Price." The article is really a **roadmap** for value pricing.

Another incredible resource to help you conceptualize and map out value pricing is the Association of Corporate Counsel's (ACC) *Value Based Fee Primer*.

There is more theory and analysis involved in the art and science of value pricing for lawyers. But remember: alternative pricing is the central focus of shifting priorities in consumers' minds, and thus also in the legal industry. Although the billable hour may never completely disappear, the use of alternative pricing models will soon be an expectation, not simply a demand, of the legal consumer. As a first mover into this arena, you will have market advantage over others who failed to pay attention to the legal world outside their office and westlaw or lexis/nexis subscription. Adopting alternative fee agreements is not only about meeting client demands and improving client relations; it's also about enticing clients by showing them you are listening and that you've responded by taking action.

CHAPTER 8:

PUTTING IT ALL TOGETHER

Many times I've sat in a conference sessions discussing the interplay of law, technology and global regulations, and the future of law, wondering how this important information I am receiving—and an understanding of its implications—will ever filter out into the ranks of the actively practicing lawyers who are already overloaded with serving their clients, paying their bills, and keeping their lives together. These are clearly urgent matters.Even as I write this final chapter, a press release has just been issued announcing that:

> *Thomson Reuters, the world's leading source of intelligent information for businesses and professionals, today announced that it has acquired Pangea3, a fast-growing legal process outsourcing (LPO) provider serving corporate legal departments and law firms worldwide.*

What does this mean? Thomson Reuters is the largest provider of research and publication services to lawyers, and which already owns a number of legal delivery systems has now acquired one of India's most successful LPOs. They have expressed their intention to open several domestic offices staffed with U.S. attorneys to provide services such as corporate due diligence, IP preparation, research and analytics,, document review, integrated discovery solutions, risk management services and more. They also staff corporate in-house legal departments, and among their clients are Fortune 500 corporations and AmLaw 250 firms.

Combining the vast array of existing LPO services of Pangea3 with the research, publishing and legal delivery systems of Thomson Reuters creates potential for significant competition within the traditional legal marketplace. Andall the rhetoric about lawyers needing to adopt twenty-first-century technology and practice management techniques or find themselves left behind just became validated, as the natural progression of the international legal business landscape took a very firm stance on US soil.

These kinds of collaborations/partnerships/buy-outs/mergers are proliferating internationally, but have until now been emerging slowly in the US, and on a relatively small scale. In other words, there was always room for competition, although time was of the essence. In "Destroying Your Own Business," Jordan Furlong asks:

> *So what are law firms, facing the same kind of threat, [Netflix vs. Blockbuster] doing these days? Merging with each other, of course: mergers <u>within the United States</u>, <u>within Canada</u> and <u>across the Atlantic</u>, with more surely*

to come. Same old response, same old thinking. Where are the law firms buying out LPOs and bringing them in-house? Where are the law firms adapting the online delivery methods of startups? Where are the law firms that recognize the peril of their position and are moving to thwart, or to transform themselves into, their smaller, swifter, hungrier new rivals? They're nowhere to be found, and that's why the future of law firms looks a lot more like Blockbuster than Netflix.

Right here, right now is the time and place to open the door to this brave new world and grab a piece of the action.

The business model that Law Practice Strategy presents is a holistic, workable solution to the challenges represented by technological advancement, globalization, and the recession. It answers the questions:

1. How do I market?
2. How do I get clients?
3. How do I serve clients?
4. How do I retain clients?
5. How do I afford all of the above?

and provides the pathway to success in these areas. Because the "legal revolution" is not about using technology, adopting alternative billing procedures, or using social media. It's about a whole new way to conceptualize what the practice of law is now and can be—which includes consideration of business practices and delivery models.

The LPS practice model is not a linear methodology, where cause and effect can be thought of as parts of 147 a chain reaction. It is a synergy of concepts that, when practiced together, creates a system that works. And yet it is also quite simple.

1. **Containing Costs.** Containing your costs will enable you to price your work to remain competitive in a marketplace where the monetary value of standardized, systematized, and packaged legal services is dropping. The way to contain your costs is to:

   • Use content marketing techniques and online networking to build visibility, presence, and interaction in the online world. Get your website up, start blogging, join online communities and networks, and use the sharing/ syndication tools that are available to you're your work visibility and your name stay familiar. Do without expensive marketers until you can afford them.

   • Use Saas cloud virtual law office platforms, law office management, legal project management, and other applications to reduce start-up and overhead expenses and create efficiency.

   • Use project management principles to strategize your case, plan and streamline your work, organize your thinking, and avoid forgetting the details, thus eliminating hours lost to chaos.

2. **Attracting Clients.** The goal here is to really understand that market forces, the progress of technology, and easy access to cheap labor is **changing the nature and process of our profession.** Your job description is being revised. It is wise to keep up with those revisions and

respond by changing your behavior—or even just your mind. In this new environment with a revised job description, attracting clients can be achieved with only minimal cost by:

- Content marketing and social media networking are incredibly powerful means to enable your clients to find you when they search for their lawyer online. Be sure that your efforts are targeted to the market you're after, and hone your blogging and social media skills to make yourself stand out.
- Be flexible in your billing practices. Potential clients are no longer willing to sign a blank check. Learn how to value your services and price them accordingly. Your willingness to work with clients on this aspect of your practice will give you a huge marketing advantage.
- Make yourself, and the legal matters, available to clients online. Like you, your clients have no extra time, and cloud tools make it as easy as possible for them to do business with you. Adopting a virtual model law firm does not rule out telephone or face-to-face meetings if and when they are necessary.

3. **Serving Clients.** In the entrepreneurial world, it is simply not possible to succeed as a start-up business without having presence online with the capability to allow customers to purchase online. Likewise, when you are providing a service, clientswant access to it online. And if you don't meet their preferred method of access, purchase and delivery, chances are your potential clients will go elsewhere to get their needs met.. The majority of

individual and small business law clients expect you to deliver quality services online. And with the sheer number of technology resources available to you, it's not just the wise thing to do, it's professional suicide not to.

- Offering fixed pricing or any alternative to open-ended hourly billing gives your clients peace of mind and creates an atmosphere of partnership and trust between you and your client.

- Did I say your clients don't have any time, either? You are serving them when you make communication and information readily accessible 24/7 via the internet. But be sure to also serve them by ensuring through due diligence that their data is secure and private and that the attorney/client privilege and confidentiality are preserved.

This will all be a kind of journey as you become more effective and efficient in running a law practice in a new and very different way. Your whole career is a journey, for that matter, it's just that this particular road hasn't been taken before. There is no case to pull up from Lexis to tell you what the rules are. Work is being conducted in the giant server farms owned by your cloud vendor. All of that data makes it on to your computer screen when you push all the right buttons. As the rules of the law practice game change, technology is enabling business as well as law firms to compete for a piece of the pie. If you're not prepared to participate in the virtual world, the chances are great that your practice will not succeed.

There is a large segment of the legal profession that find the use of technology, alternative fee arrangements, and other systems discussed here anathema to the practice of law. Our job is to consult, analyze, negotiate, and perform other services in a human capacity. That is, and always will be, true. There will always be components of what we as lawyers do that cannot be automated or outsourced. But there are also components of our profession that fit perfectly within a business structure that capitalizes on the advancements and globalization of the way business is being conducted in our society today. By employing them, we won't simply survive the recessionary effects on our profession, but also pioneer in providing easily available and inexpensive services to those who need them.

BIBLIOGRAPHY

"The ACC Value Based Fee Primer." White paper. The Association for Corporate Counsel. http://www.acc.com/advocacy/valuechallenge/toolkit/upload/acc-value-based-fee-primer.pdf Web. 23 Dec. 2010.

<http://amlawdaily.typepad.com/amlawdaily/2009/06/fmc-calls-for-help-but-few-large-firms-answer.html>.

Anderson, Michael J. "Innovate Now?" Law Firm Management—Law Firm Strategy—Law Firm Marketing. Edge International. <http://www.edge.ai/Edge-International-1057859.html>. (accessed December 21, 2010).

Baksi, Catherine. "The Best Advice on How to Prepare for a Legal Services Revolution." Web log post. *Law Society Gazette* (19 November, 2009). <http://www.lawgazette.co.uk/features/the-best-advice-how-prepare-for-legal-services-revolution>. (accessed December 21, 2010).

Bamidele, Onibalusi. "Blogging with Influence in 5 Steps." Web log post. *AriWriter* (10 May, 2010). <http://ariwriter.com/blogging-with-influence-in-5-steps/>. (accessed December 23, 2010).

Bullas, Jeff. "Is Blogging the Future of Publishing?" Web log post. Jeffbullas.com. <http://www.jeffbullas.com/2010/05/12/is-blogging-the-future-of-publishing/>. (accessed December 27, 2010).

Comodeca, James A., and Scott R. Everett. "Alternative Fee Arrangements: Risk Sharing Requires a Strong

Partnership." Web log post. Martindale.com, 7 May 2010. <http://www.martindale.com/business-law/article_Dinsmore-Shohl-LLP_1014478.htm>. (accessed December 23, 2010).

F. Cunniff, Michael S. Helfer, William D. Henderson et al., Proc. of Defining the Law Firm of the Future, New York, NY, USA. Print.

"Duane Morris LLP. UK Updates Guidance for Data-Protection Legislation with Online Code of Practice for Personal Information." Duane Morris LLP. <http://www.duanemorris.com/alerts/UK_ICO_Personal_Information_Online_Code_Practice.3732.html>. (accessed December 23, 2010).

Elon University and Pew Research Center. "Imagining the Internet." 2010. Raw data.

http://www.elon.edu/e-web/predictions/expertsurveys /2010survey/default.xhtml

Fleischman, Jay. "11 Reasons Why Content Is King." Web log post. Legal Practice Pro, 16 April, 2010. <http://www.legalpracticepro.com/online-legal-marketing-11-reasons-why-content-is-king/>. (accessed December 23, 2010).

Furlong, Jordan. "The Blind Side." Slaw, 3 April, 2010. <http://www.slaw.ca/2010/04/03/the-blind-side/>. (accessed December 21, 2010).

————. "The Boutique Exodus." Web log post, Law21, 9 February, 2010. <http://www.law21.ca/2010/02/09/the-boutique-exodus/>. (accessed December 23, 2010).

————. "Destroying Your Own Business." Web log post, Law21, 11 November, 2010. Web. <http://www.law21.ca/2010/11/11/destroying-your-own-business/>. (accessed December 23, 2010).

————. "How I Learned to Stop Worrying and Love Project Management." Web log post, Law21, 9 April, 2010. <http://www.law21.ca/2010/04/09/how-i-learned-to-stop-worrying-and-love-project-management/>. (accessed December 21, 2010).

————. "How to Compete on Price." Web log post, Law21, 25 May, 2010. <http://www.law21.ca/2010/05/25/how-to-compete-on-price/>. (accessed December 21, 2010).

————. "Metamorphosis: Five Forces Transforming the Legal Services Marketplace." *American Bar Association* (January-February, 2010). <http://www.abanet.org/lpm/magazine/articles/v36/is1/pg44.shtml>. (accessed December 23, 2010).

————. "The Platform Is Changing." Web log post, Law21, 17 March, 2010. <http://www.law21.ca/2010/03/17/the-platform-is-changing/>. (accessed December 21, 2010).

Granat, Richard. "ABA Technology EReport." *American Bar Association,* 9, no.3 (September 2010). (accessed on Internet December 23, 2010).

————. *Online Legal Services: The Future of the Profession.* White paper.

Hassett, Jim. "The Billable Hour: How Sick Is It?" Web log post, Legal Business Development, 8 September, 2010. <http://adverselling.typepad.com/how_law_firms_

sell/2010/09/the-billable-hour-how-sick-is-it.html>. (accessed December 23, 2010).

Henderson, William. "Are Law Firms Really Ready for Project Management?" Web log post, Center on the Global Legal Profession, University of Indiana, Bloomington. <http://globalprofession.law.indiana. edu/2010/07/are-law-firms-really-ready-for-project-management/>. (accessed December 21, 2010).

HubSpot.com. "The State of Inbound Lead Generation." Repr. March, 2010. (accessed on Internet December 23, 2010).

Hubspot.com. "The State of Inbound Marketing 2010." Repr. February, 2010.

Kaplan, Ari. "The Evolution of the Legal Profession." Ari Kaplan Advisors. <http://arikaplanadvisors.com/AriKaplan_DiscoverReady_EvolutionStudy_FINAL.pdf>. (accessed December 21, 2010).

Kimbro, Stephanie. "Cloud Computing in Law Practice Management." White paper, ABA Publishing, August, 2010. (accessed on Internet December 23, 2010).

———. "The Future of the Legal Profession Is Client-Centric." Web log post, Virtual Law Practice, 4 May, 2010. <http://virtuallawpractice.org/2010/05/the-future-of-the-legal-profession-is-client-centric/>. (accessed December 23, 2010).

———. "Guest Post: Ethics Considerations for the Virtual Practice of Law." Web log post, Mass. LOMAP: Law Practice Advisor, 10 August, 2010. <http://masslomap. blogspot.com/2010/08/guest-post-ethics-consider-ations-for.html>. (accessed December 23, 2010).

Kowalski, Jerome. "Alternative Fee Arrangements: Part 1." Web log post, Kowalski & Associates Blog, 31 March, 2010. <http://kowalskiandassociatesblog.com/2010/03/31/alternative-fee-arrangements-a-primer/>. (accessed December 23, 2010).

Lauritsen, Marc. *The Lawyer's Guide to Working Smarter with Knowledge Tools*. (Chicago: Law Practice Management Section, American Bar Association, 2010).

LexisNexis. "State of the Legal Industry Survey Findings." Survey results. (accessed from Internet December 27, 2010).

Liebel, Susan C. "When Large Law Firms Underestimate Lower Cost Rivals, You Win!" Solo Practice University, 3 August, 2010. <http://solopracticeuniversity.com/2010/08/03/when-large-law-firmsorganizations-underestimate-lower-cost-rivals/>. (accessed December 21, 2010)

Lurssen, Adrian. "Social Media Delivers Law Firm Content to People Who Want It." Web log post, JD Supra, 29 October, 2010. <http://scoop.jdsupra.com/2010/10/articles/law-firm-marketing/law-firms-and-social-media/>. (accessed December 23, 2010).

Miller, Amy. "Few Large Firms Answer FMC's Calls for Help." Web log post, The Am Law Daily, 15 June, 2009. Web. (accessed on Internet December 23, 2010).

New Jersey Technology Council. "The Lawyer as Entrepreneur," 2004. (Retrieved from: New Jersey Technology Council: http://jobcircle.com/career/articles/x/njtc/3018.xml).

Pangea3. "Thomson Reuters Acquires Pangea3." Pangea3, 19 November, 2010. <http://www.pangea3.com/thomson-reuters-acquires-pangea3.html>. (accessed December 23, 2010).

Scott, David M. "Brand Journalism." Web log post. Web Ink Now, 29 March, 2010. <http://www.webinknow.com/2010/03/brand-journalism-.html>. (accessed December 23, 2010).

———. *The New Rules of Marketing and PR: How to Use News Releases, Blogs, Podcasting, Viral Marketing & Online Media to Reach Buyers Directly.* (Hoboken, NJ: John Wiley & Sons, 2007).

Seyle, Donna. "Virtual Platforms and Web 2.0 Management Tools for Solos and Small Firms." *http://lawpractic-estrategy.com.* (accessed December 23, 2010).

Shepherd, Jay. "Two Kinds of Lawyers." Web log post. The Client Revolution, 5 November, 2010. http://www.clientrevolution.com/2010/11/two-kinds-of-lawyers.html (accessed December 23, 2010).

Shipley, Ruth M. "How to Cash in on Your Passion with Social Media." Web log post, Social Media Examiner, 3 May, 2010. <http://www.socialmediaexaminer.com/how-to-cash-in-on-your-passion-with-social-media/>. (accessed December 23, 2010).

Shomper, James D., and Gardner G. Courson. "Alternative Fees for Litigation: Improved Control and Higher Value." Web log post, DuPont Legal Model, <http://www.dupontlegalmodel.com/alternative-fees-for-litigation-improved-control-and-higher-value/>. (accessed December 27, 2010).

Stephenson, Correy. "Portfolio Billing: A Valuable Option for Solos, Small Firms." Web log post, Lawyers USA Online, 20 August, 2010. <http://lawyersusaonline.com/blog/2010/08/20/portfolio-billing-a-valuable-option-for-solos-small-firms/>. (accessed December 23, 2010).

Susskind, Richard E. *The End of Lawyers*. (New York: Oxford University Press, 2010).

————. "The Mainstream Revolutionary." Legal Futures, 21 September, 2010. http://www.legalfutures.co.uk/latest-news/the-mainstream-revolutionary (accessed December 21, 2010).

————. "Susskind: Fail to Embrace "Legal Process Management" and Lose Out to New Players." Legal Futures, 20 September, 2010. http://www.legalfutures.co.uk/latest-news/susskind-fail-to-embrace-legal-process-management-and-lose-out-to-new-competition. (accessed December 21, 2010).

"The Truth about Unbundled Legal Services." Web log post, Total Attorneys. <http://www.totalattorneys.com/grow-your-law-practice/the-truth-about-unbundled-legal-services/>. (accessed December 23, 2010).

University of Florida, Levin College of Law. "Case, Matter & Practice Management System Study." Legal Technology Institute, 2010. (accessed on Internet, December 23, 2010).

"Virtual Law Firm." Wikipedia, 31 August, 2010.

Wakeman, Denise. "3 Simple Ways to Repurpose Your Blog Posts for More Exposure." Web log post, Social

Media Examiner, 1 July, 2010. <http://www.socialmediaexaminer.com/3-simple-ways-to-repurpose-your-blog-posts-for-more-exposure/#comment-60183539>. (accessed December 23, 2010).

Williams, Joel. "Will a Blog Really Help Me Promote My Business?" Web log post, Blog Tech Guy, 26 April, 2010. <http://blogtechguy.com/1675/will-a-blog-really-help-me-promote-my-business/>. (accessed December 23, 2010).

Woldow, Pam. "Stop Complaining & DO Something!" Web log post, At The Intersection, 7 September, 2010. <http://pwoldow.wordpress.com/2010/09/07/stop-complaining-do-something/>. (accessed December 21, 2010).

Wurtzel, E. "Tough Times for Big Law." The Wall Street Journal, 14 December, 2009. http://online.wsj.com/article/SB10001424052748704240504574586431109327544.html

WEB RESOURCES

Agile Framework: http://www.ccpace.com/Resources/documents/AgileProjectManagement.pdf

Eversheds: http://www.eversheds.com/clientsrevolution

Forrester: http://www.forrester.com/rb/research

Jaskie Webinar: http://www.brighttalk.com/channel/231JDSupra: http://www.jdsupra.com/

Law Firm Evolution: Brave New World or Business as Usual?: http://www.law.georgetown.edu/legalprofession/documents/LAWFIRMEVOLUTION02252010.

Legal Advice on a Budget: http://online.wsj.com/article/SB10001424052748703615104575329193640764492.html

The Legal Implications of Cloud Computing: http://www.infolawgroup.com/2009/08/tags/security/legal-implications-of-cloud-computing-part-one-the-basics-and-framing-the-issues/

Martindale-Hubbell Connected: http://community.martindale.com/SignIn.aspx

MyLegal: http://www.mylegal.com/default.aspx

Pricing on Purpose: How to Implement Value Pricing in Your Firm: http://www.journalofaccountancy.com/Issues/2009/Jun/20091530.htm

Project Counsel: http://www.projectcounsel.com/?p=623

www.ingramcontent.com/pod-product-compliance
Lightning Source LLC
Chambersburg PA
CBHW060030210326
41520CB00009B/1068